KETO *FOR* CANCER

RECIPES COOKBOOK

A 28-Day Meal Plan with Simple, Delicious Recipes and Nutritional Strategies fora metabolic and Low-Carb Lifestyle

Dr. Kevin Abbott

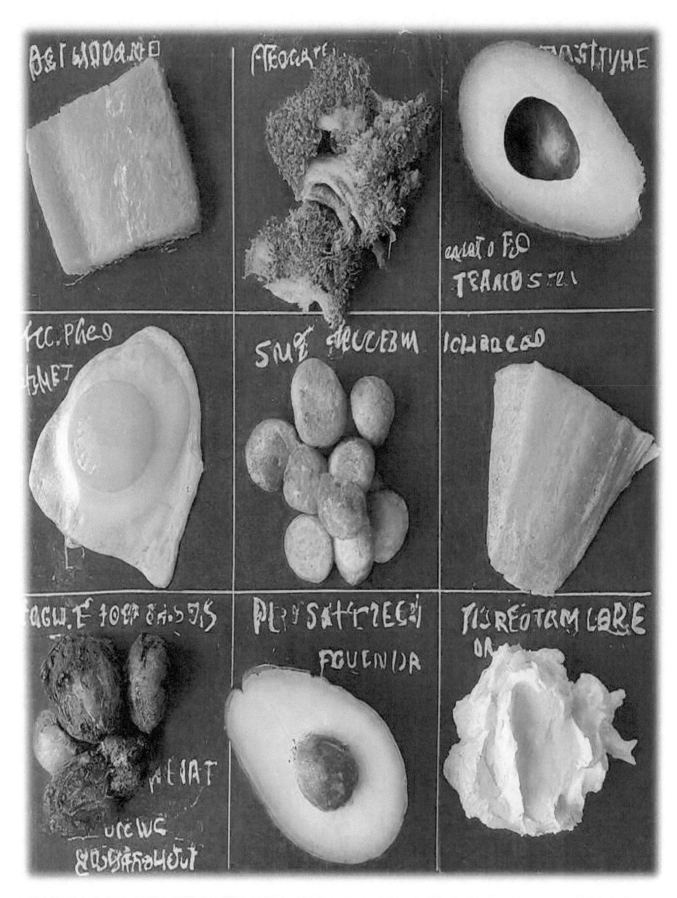

Disclaimer: These recipes are not intended to heal or cure cancer. They are healthy, keto-friendly meal options that may support overall wellness when included in a balanced ketogenic diet during cancer treatment and management under proper medical supervision. Always consult with your oncology team before making significant dietary changes, as individual needs may vary based on cancer type, treatment plan, and overall health status.

If approved by your healthcare providers, incorporating these keto-friendly recipes into your diet could potentially provide nutritional support during cancer treatment by supplying essential nutrients, healthy fats, lean proteins, fiber, and antioxidants. However, they should be viewed as complementary to, not a replacement for, conventional cancer therapies prescribed by your oncologists and cancer specialists.

I wish you all the best in this journey

Table of Contents

Introduction

Cancer.

A word that strikes fear into the hearts of many. A diagnosis that shatters lives and leaves families grasping for answers. I've witnessed this firsthand, not just as a physician, but as a fellow human being.

My name is Dr. Kevin Abbott, and I've dedicated my career to the pursuit of healing. As an oncologist, I've seen the toll cancer takes on my patients and their loved ones. It's a battle fought on many fronts, and every weapon in our arsenal is crucial.

In recent years, I've become increasingly fascinated by the potential of the ketogenic diet as a powerful ally in the fight against cancer. The science behind it is compelling, and the stories of patients who have experienced remarkable benefits are truly inspiring.

One such patient, Emily, a vibrant young woman with a radiant smile, was facing a daunting diagnosis. Traditional treatments had taken their toll, leaving her exhausted and depleted. But when Emily embraced the ketogenic diet, something incredible happened. Her energy returned, her symptoms improved, and she regained a sense of control over her health.

Emily's story ignited a spark in me. It reinforced my belief that nutrition plays a vital role in cancer care, and that the ketogenic diet holds a unique promise for patients seeking a holistic approach to healing.

This book is born out of that passion. It's a comprehensive guide to the ketogenic diet for cancer patients, meticulously researched and thoughtfully crafted to empower you on your journey. I've poured my knowledge and experience into these pages, along with the wisdom of leading experts in the field.

Inside, you'll discover:

- The science behind keto and how it works to support your body during cancer treatment.

- Practical tips for transitioning to a ketogenic lifestyle, including meal planning, grocery shopping, and navigating social situations.

- Over 100 delicious and easy-to-follow recipes that will nourish your body and delight your senses, even when your appetite is waning.

- Guidance on incorporating nutritional supplements that may benefit cancer patients on a ketogenic diet.

- Strategies for managing other health conditions alongside cancer, such as diabetes, heart disease, and high blood pressure.

- Inspiring stories of hope and resilience from other keto warriors who have walked this path before you.

This book is not a substitute for medical advice, but rather a complementary tool to help you make informed decisions about your health. It's my hope that it will provide you with knowledge, support, and a renewed sense of empowerment as you navigate the challenges of cancer treatment.

You are not alone. There is a growing community of individuals who are embracing the ketogenic diet as a way to reclaim their health and fight back against cancer. This book is your invitation to join them.

So let's turn the page together and embark on this journey of healing and hope. With the ketogenic diet as your ally, you can face cancer with courage, resilience, and the knowledge that you are doing everything in your power to support your body's innate ability to heal.

Chapter 1: The Science Behind Keto

Now, I know what you're thinking: "Science? Ugh, boring!" But trust me, understanding the basics of the ketogenic diet isn't just about memorizing facts and figures. It's about discovering how this way of eating can truly transform your body into a cancer-fighting machine.

What exactly is ketosis?

So, what exactly is ketosis? Imagine your body as a car. Normally, it runs on gasoline (carbs), which is

readily available and easy to burn. But when you switch to the keto diet, you're essentially changing the fuel source to diesel (fat).

At first, your body might sputter and cough a bit as it adjusts to this new fuel. But once it gets the hang of it, it runs smoother, cleaner, and more efficiently. That's ketosis.

Ketosis is a metabolic state where your body shifts from burning carbs for energy to burning fat. This happens when you drastically reduce your carbohydrate intake and increase your consumption of healthy fats. Your liver then starts converting fat into molecules called ketones, which become your primary fuel source.

"Okay, but why is this important for cancer patients?" you might ask.

Well, research suggests that cancer cells have a harder time using ketones for energy compared to normal cells. By depriving them of their preferred fuel source (glucose from carbs), you can potentially slow their growth and make them more vulnerable to treatment.

Think of it like cutting off the enemy's supply lines. By switching to keto, you're essentially starving the cancer cells while nourishing your healthy cells. Pretty amazing, right?

But the benefits of ketosis go beyond just cancer. It can also help reduce inflammation, stabilize blood sugar levels, boost energy, and even improve cognitive function. It's like giving your entire body a tune-up!

Now, I don't want to overwhelm you with too much science, but it's important to understand the basic principles behind the ketogenic diet. In the next few sections, we'll dive deeper into the different types of ketones, the role of macronutrients (fat, protein, and carbs), and how to monitor your progress to make sure you're staying in ketosis.

So grab a cup of tea (or maybe a bulletproof coffee!), get comfy, and let's explore the incredible world of keto together.

Why Keto for Cancer? The Metabolic Advantage

Think of cancer cells like spoiled kids with a sweet tooth. They thrive on sugar, or more specifically, glucose, which comes from the carbohydrates we eat. But what if we could cut off their candy supply? That's where the ketogenic diet comes in.

By drastically reducing carb intake and increasing healthy fats, we force our bodies to switch from burning sugar to burning fat for fuel. This metabolic shift is like flipping a switch inside our cells, creating an environment that's much less hospitable to cancer.

You see, cancer cells are picky eaters. They lack the machinery to efficiently use fat for energy, so when we deprive them of their favorite sugary treats, they start to wither. It's like taking away a kid's candy and replacing it with broccoli – they're not going to be happy about it!

This metabolic advantage is what makes the ketogenic diet so intriguing for cancer patients. It's not just about starving the cancer cells, though; it's also about nourishing the healthy cells in our bodies with a steady supply of ketones, a superfuel derived from fat. Ketones are not only a more efficient source of energy, but they also have anti-inflammatory properties that can help reduce the damage caused by cancer and its treatments.

So, by adopting a ketogenic lifestyle, we're essentially creating a double whammy against cancer: starving the bad guys while fueling the good guys. It's a powerful approach that can complement conventional treatments and improve overall health and well-being.

Macronutrients: Your Keto Building Blocks

Now, let's talk about the building blocks of the ketogenic diet: macronutrients. These are the nutrients that provide our bodies with energy, and they come in three main categories: carbohydrates, protein, and fat.

Think of them as the ingredients in a recipe. You need the right balance of each to create a delicious and nutritious meal. Similarly, the ketogenic diet requires a specific ratio of macronutrients to induce ketosis and reap its benefits.

Carbohydrates: On keto, we severely limit carbs. This means saying goodbye to bread, pasta, rice, sugar, and most fruits. While it might sound daunting at first, it's essential for switching your body into fat-burning mode.

Protein: Protein is important for building and repairing tissues, so we don't want to skimp on it. But we also don't want to overdo it, as excess protein can be converted into glucose, kicking us out of ketosis. We'll aim for a moderate amount of protein, focusing on high-quality sources like meat, fish, eggs, and dairy.

Fat: This is the star of the show on keto! Healthy fats like avocado, nuts, seeds, olive oil, and coconut oil become our primary source of energy. They keep us feeling full and satisfied, while also providing essential nutrients for our bodies.

Now, don't worry about memorizing exact numbers just yet. We'll dive deeper into the ideal macronutrient ratios for cancer patients in the next sections. For now, just remember that keto is all about prioritizing healthy fats and limiting carbs. It's a delicious and satisfying way of eating that can have a profound impact on your health and well-being, especially if you're facing the challenges of cancer.

Macronutrient Calculation: Your Personalized Keto Roadmap

Think of a macro calculator as your trusty GPS for the ketogenic journey. It's a tool that helps you determine the exact amounts of carbohydrates, protein, and fat you need to eat each day to reach and maintain ketosis.

But why do we need this personalized roadmap? Well, just like every car has a different fuel efficiency, every body has unique needs based on factors like age, weight, activity level, and individual metabolism. A macro calculator takes these factors into account to create a tailored plan just for you.

Here's how it works:

1. **Gather your information:** You'll need to input your age, gender, weight, height, and activity level. Some calculators may also ask about your goals (weight loss, maintenance, muscle gain) and any underlying health conditions.

2. **Let the calculator do the math:** The calculator uses this information to estimate your total daily energy expenditure (TDEE), which is the number of calories your body burns in a day. It then calculates your macronutrient needs based on the standard ketogenic ratio:

   o   70-75% of calories from fat

   o   20-25% of calories from protein

   o   5-10% of calories from carbs

3. **Get your personalized macros:** The calculator will provide you with the ideal number of grams of carbs, protein, and fat you should consume each day to achieve ketosis.

4. **Track your intake:** You can use a food tracking app or simply keep a journal to monitor your daily macronutrient intake. This will help you stay on track and ensure you're hitting your targets.

Now, here's a simple example to illustrate how it works:

Let's say your macro calculator determines that you need 1500 calories per day to maintain your current weight. Based on the standard keto ratio, your macros would be approximately:

- Fat: 116 grams (75% of calories)

- Protein: 75 grams (20% of calories)

- Carbs: 19 grams (5% of calories)

This means you'll need to focus on incorporating plenty of healthy fats into your meals, while keeping your carb intake very low. You can use this information to plan your meals, choose keto-friendly recipes, and make informed decisions when you're out and about.

These are just guidelines. Your individual needs may vary, and it's important to listen to your body and adjust your macros as needed.

I recommend using a reputable online macro calculator or consulting with a registered dietitian who specializes in the ketogenic diet for cancer patients or you can personally contact me through this email(Digitron10000@gmail.com). We can help you fine-tune your macros and provide personalized guidance throughout your journey.

Chapter 2: Getting Started with Keto

Alright, so you're ready to dive into the world of keto and harness its power for your health. That's fantastic! But before we jump into meal plans and recipes, let's talk about how to make the transition as smooth as possible. Trust me, starting a new way of eating can be a bit bumpy, but with a few tips and tricks, you'll be cruising along in ketosis before you know it.

Transitioning into Ketosis: Tips for a Smooth Start

Think of transitioning to keto like changing gears in a car. You wouldn't slam on the brakes and expect a smooth ride, right? The same goes for your body. A gradual shift is key to avoiding the dreaded "keto flu" and ensuring a comfortable transition.

Here are some tips to get you started:

1. **Start by cleaning out your pantry:** Say goodbye to sugary snacks, processed foods, bread, pasta, and rice. It might be tough at first, but remember, it's for the greater good! Stock up on keto-friendly staples like healthy fats, proteins, and low-carb veggies.

2. **Ease into it:** Instead of going cold turkey on carbs, gradually reduce your intake over a few days or weeks. This will give your body time to adjust and minimize any unpleasant side effects.

3. **Stay hydrated:** Drinking plenty of water is crucial on keto. It helps flush out toxins, prevents dehydration, and can even curb cravings. Aim for at least 8 glasses of water a day, and consider adding electrolytes to replenish those lost through increased urination.

4. **Don't be afraid of fat:** Fat is your friend on keto! Embrace healthy fats like avocados, nuts, seeds, olive oil, and fatty fish. They'll keep you feeling full and satisfied, while also providing essential nutrients.

5. **Monitor your electrolytes:** When you first start keto, your body excretes more water and electrolytes, which can lead to fatigue, headaches, and muscle cramps. Supplementing with electrolytes like sodium, potassium, and magnesium can help alleviate these symptoms.

6. **Be patient:** It can take a few days or even weeks for your body to fully adapt to ketosis. Don't get discouraged if you don't see results immediately. Stick with it, trust the process, and soon you'll be reaping the rewards of this incredible way of eating.

7. **Listen to your body:** Everyone's experience with keto is unique. Pay attention to how your body feels and adjust your macros or food choices as needed. Don't hesitate to reach out to a healthcare professional or registered dietitian for personalized guidance.

Transitioning to keto is a journey, not a race. Be kind to yourself, celebrate your small victories, and don't be afraid to ask for help when you need it. With the right mindset and these helpful tips, you'll be well on your way to achieving your health goals and thriving on the ketogenic diet.

Common Mistakes to Avoid on the Ketogenic Journey

Think of the ketogenic diet as a scenic road trip. It's an exciting adventure, but like any journey, there can be a few bumps along the way. Avoiding these common pitfalls will help ensure a smooth and successful ride towards better health.

1. **Fear of Fat:** This might seem counterintuitive, but many people starting keto are hesitant to fully embrace fat. Remember, fat is your primary fuel source on this diet! Don't be afraid to load up on healthy fats like avocados, olive oil, nuts, and fatty fish.

2. **Skimping on Veggies:** It's easy to get caught up in the excitement of bacon and butter, but don't forget about your veggies! They're packed with essential nutrients and fiber, which is important for digestion and overall health. Aim for a variety of non-starchy vegetables like leafy greens, broccoli, cauliflower, and zucchini.

3. **Ignoring Electrolytes:** As your body adjusts to ketosis, it flushes out excess water and electrolytes. This can lead to the dreaded "keto flu," which is characterized by fatigue, headaches,

and muscle cramps. Replenish those electrolytes by drinking plenty of water, adding a pinch of salt to your meals, and considering electrolyte supplements.

4. **Overdoing Protein:** While protein is important, too much can actually kick you out of ketosis. Your body can convert excess protein into glucose, which is the very fuel you're trying to avoid. Stick to moderate amounts of protein, focusing on high-quality sources like meat, fish, eggs, and dairy.

5. **Falling for "Keto" Treats:** Just because a product is labeled "keto-friendly" doesn't mean it's healthy. Many processed keto snacks are loaded with artificial sweeteners and unhealthy ingredients. Stick to whole, unprocessed foods as much as possible, and enjoy occasional treats in moderation.

6. **Not Tracking:** In the beginning, it's helpful to track your food intake to ensure you're hitting your macro targets and staying in ketosis. This doesn't have to be a lifelong habit, but it can be a valuable tool for learning the ropes and establishing healthy habits.

7. **Comparing Yourself to Others:** Everyone's keto journey is unique. Don't get discouraged if your progress looks different from someone else's. Focus on your own goals, celebrate your wins, and remember that consistency is key.

Tracking Your Progress

Think of tracking your progress as checking your map along the way. It helps you see how far you've come, identify any detours, and stay on course towards your destination.

Here are some ways to track your progress on keto:

- **Ketone Levels:** You can use urine strips, blood meters, or breath analyzers to measure your ketone levels. This will tell you if you're in ketosis and how deep you are.

- **Weight and Measurements:** Keep track of your weight, waist circumference, and other measurements to see how your body composition is changing. Remember, weight loss isn't the only goal on keto.

- **Energy Levels and Mood:** Pay attention to how you feel. Are you feeling more energetic, focused, and clear-headed? These are all positive signs that your body is adapting to keto.

- **Hunger and Cravings:** As you get fat-adapted, your appetite should naturally decrease, and cravings for sugary foods should subside.

- **Non-Scale Victories:** Don't forget to celebrate the non-scale victories like improved sleep, better digestion, clearer skin, or increased mental clarity.

By tracking your progress, you'll gain valuable insights into how your body is responding to the ketogenic diet. This information can help you make adjustments, stay motivated, and ultimately achieve your health goals. Remember, it's a journey, not a race. Enjoy the ride and celebrate every milestone along the way!

Chapter 3: The 28-Day Keto Meal Plan

Congratulations on taking the first step towards a healthier you! This Meal Plan marks the beginning of your ketogenic journey, a time of transition and discovery. As your body adjusts to using fat as its primary fuel source, you may experience some initial side effects like fatigue, headaches, or cravings. Don't worry, this is completely normal and often referred to as the "keto flu."

But fear not, I've designed this week's meal plan to ease you into ketosis gently, providing your body with the nutrients it needs to thrive while minimizing any discomfort. The recipes are simple, delicious, and packed with healthy fats to keep you feeling full and satisfied.

The 28-Day Keto Meal Plan

Week 1: Kickstarting Ketosis

- Focus: Gentle transition, focus on healthy fats, moderate protein, and very low carbs.

Day	Breakfasts	Lunch	Dinner	Snacks
1	Avocado Egg Salad Stuffed Tomatoes	Salmon Salad with Lemon-Dill Dressing	Chicken Curry with Cauliflower Rice	Olives, Almonds, Hard-Boiled Eggs
2	Bacon and Spinach Frittata	Zesty Shrimp Salad	Turkey Meatballs with Zucchini Noodles	Berries with Whipped Cream, Celery/Almond Butter
3	Coconut Flour Pancakes with Berries	Tuna Salad Lettuce Wraps	Beef Stir-Fry with Broccoli and Peppers	Macadamia Nuts, Avocado Deviled Eggs
4	Keto Green Smoothie	Chicken Caesar Salad	Pork Chops with Roasted Brussels Sprouts	String Cheese, Sugar-Free Jello
5	Chia Seed Pudding with Coconut Flakes	Leftover Chicken Curry	Baked Salmon with Asparagus	Cucumber Slices with Cream Cheese, Beef Jerky
6	Leftovers	Leftovers	Leftovers	Mixed Nuts and Seeds
7	Keto Breakfast Salad	Smoked Salmon Omelette	Salmon with Lemon-Dill Sauce	Roasted Radishes with Herbs

- Focus: Increase variety, incorporate more vegetables, continue monitoring for any keto flu symptoms.

Day	Breakfasts	Lunch	Dinner	Snacks
1	Keto Breakfast Skillet	Cheeseburger Salad	Creamy Tuscan Garlic Chicken	Kale Chips
2	Mushroom and Cheese Scramble	Leftover Cauliflower Mac and Cheese	Garlic Butter Steak Bites/Mushrooms	Pork Rinds
3	Baked Avocado Boats with Eggs	Tuna Stuffed Avocados	One-Pan Roasted Chicken/Vegetables	Berries with Whipped Cream/Mascarpone
4	Keto Smoothie	Chicken Salad with Avocado Mayo	Beef Stroganoff (with zoodles)	Coconut Chips
5	Sausage and Egg Muffins	Leftover Beef Stroganoff	Lamb Chops with Mint Pesto	Celery Sticks/Almond Butter
6	Leftovers	Leftovers	Leftovers	Mixed Nuts and Seeds
7	Keto Breakfast Salad	Smoked Salmon Omelette	Salmon with Lemon-Dill Sauce	Roasted Radishes with Herbs

- Focus: Explore new recipes, focus on nutrient density, continue to listen to your body's needs.

Day	Breakfasts	Lunch	Dinner	Snacks
1	Keto Smoothie	Portobello Mushroom Pizzas	Garlic Butter Shrimp	Celery Sticks/Almond Butter
2	Leftover Keto Smoothie	Zucchini Lasagna	Creamy Tuscan Chicken Skillet	Hard-Boiled Eggs
3	Bacon and Spinach Frittata	Vegetable Frittata	Coconut Curry Chicken Soup	Sugar-Free Jello/Whipped Cream
4	Chia Seed Pudding	Cream of Mushroom Soup	Fish Tacos with Cabbage Shells	Kale Chips
5	Almond Flour Muffins	Stuffed Bell Peppers/Cauliflower	Pan-Seared Scallops/Cauliflower Risotto	Pork Rinds
6	Leftovers	Leftovers	Leftovers	Mixed Nuts and Seeds
7	Your Choice!	Your Choice!	Your Choice!	Your Choice!

Week 4: Maintaining Keto for Long-Term Health

- Focus: Continue exploring recipes, focus on sustainability, make keto a lifestyle.

Day	Breakfasts	Lunch	Dinner	Snacks
1	Zucchini Bread Omelette	Shrimp Scampi with Zucchini Noodles	Meatloaf Muffins	Cucumber Slices/Cream Cheese
2	Bone Broth with Egg Drop	Leftover Shrimp Scampi	Shepherd's Pie (cauliflower mash)	Hard-Boiled Eggs
3	Keto Coconut Porridge/Nuts/Seeds	Chicken Fajita Bowls	Chili Con Carne (no beans)	Sugar-Free Jello with Whipped Cream
4	Leftover Keto Porridge	Leftover Chicken Fajitas	Korean Beef Bowls	Kale Chips
5	Avocado Egg Salad	Cauliflower Mac and Cheese	Baked Cod with Lemon and Herbs	Pork Rinds
6	Leftovers	Leftovers	Leftovers	Mixed Nuts and Seeds
7	Keto Egg Muffins/Spinach/Feta	Eggplant Parmesan (almond flour breaded)	One-Pan Baked Fish/Mediterranean Veg	Roasted Brussels Sprouts with Bacon

Chapter 4: Ketogenic Diet Recipes for Cancer Patients

Disclaimer: These recipes are not intended to heal or cure cancer. They are healthy, keto-friendly meal options that may support overall wellness when included in a balanced ketogenic diet during cancer treatment and management under proper medical supervision. Always consult with your oncology team before making significant dietary changes, as individual needs may vary based on cancer type, treatment plan, and overall health status.

If approved by your healthcare providers, incorporating these keto-friendly recipes into your diet could potentially provide nutritional support during cancer treatment by supplying essential nutrients, healthy fats, lean proteins, fiber, and antioxidants. However, they should be viewed as complementary to, not a replacement for, conventional cancer therapies prescribed by your oncologists and cancer specialists.

Breakfast Recipes

Avocado Egg Salad

Prep time: 10 minutes

Nutritional values (per serving): Calories: 310, Fat: 27g, Protein: 12g, Carbs: 5g

Ingredients:

- ✓ 2 hard-boiled eggs, chopped
- ✓ 1 ripe avocado, mashed
- ✓ 1 tablespoon mayonnaise (optional)
- ✓ 1/2 teaspoon Dijon mustard
- ✓ 1/4 cup chopped celery
- ✓ 1/4 cup chopped red onion
- ✓ Salt and pepper to taste

Instructions:

1. Combine all ingredients in a bowl.
2. Mash with a fork until desired consistency is reached.
3. Season with salt and pepper.
4. Serve on lettuce leaves, in avocado halves, or with cucumber slices.

Bacon and Spinach Frittata

Prep time: 15 minutes

Cook time: 20 minutes

Nutritional values (per serving): Calories: 280, Fat: 22g, Protein: 15g, Carbs: 4g

Ingredients:

- ✓ 4 slices bacon, diced
- ✓ 1/2 cup chopped onion
- ✓ 2 cups fresh spinach
- ✓ 6 eggs
- ✓ 1/4 cup heavy cream
- ✓ 1/4 cup shredded cheddar cheese
- ✓ Salt and pepper to taste

Instructions:

1. Preheat oven to 350°F (175°C).
2. Cook bacon in a skillet until crisp. Remove and set aside.
3. Sauté onion in bacon grease until softened. Add spinach and cook until wilted.
4. Whisk together eggs and heavy cream. Season with salt and pepper.
5. Stir in cooked bacon, onion, and spinach. Pour into a greased baking dish.
6. Sprinkle with cheese and bake for 20 minutes, or until set.

Smoked Salmon Omelette

Prep time: 5 minutes

Cook time: 10 minutes

Nutritional values (per serving): Calories: 350, Fat: 28g, Protein: 20g, Carbs: 3g

Ingredients:

- 2 eggs
- 1 tablespoon butter
- 2 ounces smoked salmon, chopped
- 1/4 cup chopped red onion
- 1 tablespoon chopped fresh dill
- Salt and pepper to taste

Instructions:

1. Whisk together eggs, salt, and pepper.
2. Melt butter in a skillet over medium heat.
3. Pour in eggs and cook, stirring occasionally, until almost set.
4. Sprinkle with smoked salmon, red onion, and dill.
5. Fold omelette in half and cook for another minute.

Keto Breakfast Casserole

Prep time: 20 minutes

Cook time: 30 minutes

Nutritional values (per serving): Calories: 380, Fat: 30g, Protein: 25g, Carbs: 5g

Ingredients:

- 1 pound breakfast sausage, browned and crumbled
- 1/2 cup chopped onion
- 1/2 cup chopped green bell pepper
- 1 cup cauliflower rice

- 6 eggs
- 1 cup heavy cream
- 1/2 cup shredded cheddar cheese
- Salt and pepper to taste

Instructions:

1. Preheat oven to 350°F (175°C).
2. Sauté onion and bell pepper in a skillet until softened.
3. Combine sausage, vegetables, cauliflower rice, eggs, heavy cream, and cheese in a bowl. Season with salt and pepper.
4. Pour into a greased baking dish and bake for 30 minutes, or until golden brown and set.

Mushroom and Cheese Scramble

- **Prep time:** 5 minutes
- **Cook time:** 10 minutes
- **Nutritional values (per serving):** Calories: 250, Fat: 20g, Protein: 15g, Carbs: 3g

Ingredients:

- 2 eggs
- 1 tablespoon butter
- 1/2 cup sliced mushrooms
- 1/4 cup shredded cheddar cheese
- Salt and pepper to taste

Instructions:

1. Melt butter in a skillet over medium heat.
2. Add mushrooms and cook until softened.

Sausage and Egg Muffins (with clean, nitrate-free sausage)

Prep time: 10 minutes

Cook time: 20 minutes

Nutritional values (per muffin): Calories: 220, Fat: 18g, Protein: 10g, Carbs: 2g

Ingredients:

- 1 pound nitrate-free breakfast sausage
- 6 large eggs
- 1/4 cup heavy cream
- 1/4 cup shredded cheddar cheese
- Salt and pepper to taste

Instructions:

1. Preheat oven to 375°F (190°C). Grease a muffin tin.
2. Cook sausage in a skillet until browned. Drain excess grease.
3. Whisk together eggs and heavy cream. Season with salt and pepper.
4. Divide sausage evenly among muffin cups.
5. Pour egg mixture over sausage, filling each cup about 3/4 full.
6. Sprinkle with cheese.
7. Bake for 20-25 minutes, or until golden brown and set.

Zucchini Bread Omelette

Prep time: 10 minutes

Cook time: 10 minutes

Nutritional values (per serving): Calories: 290, Fat: 24g, Protein: 12g, Carbs: 5g

Ingredients:

- 2 eggs
- 1 tablespoon butter
- 1/2 cup grated zucchini
- 1/4 cup almond flour
- 1/4 teaspoon baking powder
- 1/4 teaspoon cinnamon
- Pinch of nutmeg
- Salt and pepper to taste

Instructions:

1. Whisk together eggs, zucchini, almond flour, baking powder, cinnamon, nutmeg, salt, and pepper.
2. Melt butter in a skillet over medium heat.
3. Pour in egg mixture and cook, stirring occasionally, until almost set.
4. Fold omelette in half and cook for another minute.

Bone Broth with Egg Drop

Prep time: 5 minutes

Cook time: 10 minutes

Nutritional values (per serving): Calories: 150, Fat: 10g, Protein: 10g, Carbs: 2g

Ingredients:

- 2 cups bone broth
- 2 eggs
- 1 tablespoon chopped chives
- Salt and pepper to taste

Instructions:

1. Heat bone broth in a saucepan.
2. Whisk eggs in a separate bowl.
3. Slowly drizzle eggs into hot broth while stirring constantly.
4. Cook until eggs are cooked through.
5. Season with salt, pepper, and chives.

Keto Breakfast Salad

Prep time: 15 minutes

Nutritional values (per serving): Calories: 400, Fat: 30g, Protein: 20g, Carbs: 5g

Ingredients:

- 4 cups mixed greens
- 4 ounces grilled chicken or salmon, chopped
- 1/2 avocado, sliced
- 1/4 cup chopped walnuts
- 1/4 cup crumbled goat cheese
- Keto-friendly dressing of your choice

- **Instructions:**

1. Combine all ingredients in a bowl.
2. Toss with dressing just before serving.

Leftover Chicken with Avocado

Prep time: 5 minutes

Nutritional values (per serving): Calories: 350, Fat: 25g, Protein: 30g, Carbs: 5g

Ingredients:

- 1 cup cooked chicken, shredded
- 1/2 avocado, sliced
- Salt and pepper to taste

Instructions:

1. Combine chicken and avocado in a bowl.
2. Season with salt and pepper.

Chia Seed Pudding

Prep time: 5 minutes

Chill time: 2 hours (or overnight)

Nutritional values (per serving): Calories: 250, Fat: 18g, Protein: 6g, Carbs: 8g

Ingredients:

- 1/4 cup chia seeds
- 1 cup unsweetened almond milk

- 1 tablespoon sweetener of your choice (e.g., stevia, erythritol)
- 1/2 teaspoon vanilla extract
- Optional toppings: berries, nuts, seeds, coconut flakes

Instructions:

1. Combine chia seeds, almond milk, sweetener, and vanilla in a jar or bowl.
2. Stir well to combine and let sit for 5 minutes.
3. Stir again to break up any clumps.
4. Refrigerate for at least 2 hours, or overnight, until thickened.
5. Top with desired toppings before serving.

Almond Flour Muffins

Prep time: 15 minutes

Cook time: 20 minutes

Nutritional values (per muffin): Calories: 180, Fat: 15g, Protein: 6g, Carbs: 4g

Ingredients:

- 1 1/2 cups almond flour
- 1/4 cup coconut flour
- 1 teaspoon baking powder
- 1/2 teaspoon baking soda
- 1/4 teaspoon salt
- 1/2 cup melted coconut oil or butter
- 1/2 cup unsweetened almond milk

- 2 eggs
- 1 teaspoon vanilla extract
- 1/4 cup sweetener of your choice (e.g., stevia, erythritol)
- Optional add-ins: berries, nuts, chocolate chips

- **Instructions:**

1. Preheat oven to 350°F (175°C). Line a muffin tin with paper liners.
2. In a large bowl, combine almond flour, coconut flour, baking powder, baking soda, and salt.
3. In a separate bowl, whisk together melted coconut oil, almond milk, eggs, vanilla extract, and sweetener.
4. Pour wet ingredients into dry ingredients and mix until just combined. Do not overmix.
5. Fold in any desired add-ins.
6. Divide batter evenly among muffin cups.
7. Bake for 20-25 minutes, or until golden brown and a toothpick inserted into the center comes out clean.

Keto Smoothie (with low-sugar fruits/veggies):

Prep time: 5 minutes

Nutritional values (per serving): Calories: 300, Fat: 25g, Protein: 10g, Carbs: 5g

Ingredients:

- 1 cup unsweetened almond milk or coconut milk
- 1/2 cup spinach or kale
- 1/4 avocado
- 1 tablespoon nut butter
- 1 scoop protein powder (optional)
- 1/4 teaspoon vanilla extract
- 1/4 cup crushed ice

Instructions:

1. Combine all ingredients in a blender.
2. Blend until smooth and creamy.

Berries with Whipped Cream:

Prep time: 5 minutes

Nutritional values (per serving): Calories: 200, Fat: 18g, Protein: 2g, Carbs: 7g

Ingredients:

- 1 cup mixed berries (strawberries, raspberries, blueberries)
- 1/2 cup heavy whipping cream
- 1/4 teaspoon vanilla extract

Instructions:

1. In a small bowl, whip heavy cream and vanilla extract until soft peaks form.
2. Divide berries among bowls and top with whipped cream.

Baked Avocado Boats with Eggs:

Prep time: 5 minutes

Cook time: 15 minutes

Nutritional values (per serving): Calories: 300, Fat: 25g, Protein: 12g, Carbs: 5g

- **Ingredients:**
- 2 avocados, halved and pitted
- 4 eggs
- Salt and pepper to taste
- Optional toppings: crumbled bacon, chopped chives, shredded cheese

Instructions:

1. Preheat oven to 400°F (200°C).
2. Scoop out a small portion of avocado flesh from each half to make room for the egg.
3. Crack one egg into each avocado half.
4. Season with salt and pepper.
5. Bake for 15-20 minutes, or until eggs are set to your liking.
6. Top with desired toppings before serving.

Cauliflower Hash Browns with Eggs:

Prep time: 10 minutes

Cook time: 20 minutes

Nutritional values (per serving): Calories: 350, Fat: 28g, Protein: 15g, Carbs: 6g

Ingredients:

- 1 head cauliflower, grated
- 1/4 cup almond flour
- 1 egg, beaten
- 1 tablespoon olive oil
- Salt and pepper to taste
- 2 eggs, fried or scrambled

Instructions:

1. Preheat oven to 400°F (200°C).
2. Combine grated cauliflower, almond flour, egg, olive oil, salt, and pepper in a bowl. Mix well.
3. Form into patties and place on a baking sheet lined with parchment paper.
4. Bake for 15-20 minutes per side, or until golden brown and crispy.
5. Serve with fried or scrambled eggs.

Keto Coconut Porridge with Nuts and Seeds:

Prep time: 5 minutes

Cook time: 10 minutes

Nutritional values (per serving): Calories: 300, Fat: 25g, Protein: 8g, Carbs: 6g

Ingredients:

- 1/2 cup unsweetened shredded coconut
- 1/2 cup coconut milk
- 1/4 cup water
- 1/4 teaspoon vanilla extract
- Pinch of salt
- Optional toppings: berries, nuts, seeds, cinnamon

Instructions:

1. Combine shredded coconut, coconut milk, water, vanilla extract, and salt in a saucepan.
2. Bring to a simmer over medium heat, stirring frequently.
3. Cook for 5-7 minutes, or until thickened.
4. Top with desired toppings before serving.

Smoked Salmon and Cream Cheese Cucumber Bites:

Prep time: 10 minutes

Nutritional values (per bite): Calories: 80, Fat: 7g, Protein: 3g, Carbs: 1g

Ingredients:

- 1 cucumber, sliced
- 4 ounces smoked salmon, sliced
- 4 ounces cream cheese, softened
- Fresh dill, for garnish

Instructions:

1. Top each cucumber slice with a dollop of cream cheese and a piece of smoked salmon.
2. Garnish with fresh dill.

Keto Egg Muffins with Spinach and Feta:

Prep time: 10 minutes

Cook time: 20 minutes

Nutritional values (per muffin): Calories: 150, Fat: 12g, Protein: 8g, Carbs: 2g

Ingredients:

- 6 eggs
- 1/2 cup chopped spinach
- 1/4 cup crumbled feta cheese
- Salt and pepper to taste

Instructions:

1. Preheat oven to 350°F (175°C). Grease a muffin tin.
2. Whisk together eggs, spinach, feta, salt, and pepper.
3. Divide mixture evenly among muffin cups.

4. Bake for 20 minutes, or until set.

Keto Breakfast Skillet with Sausage and Vegetables:

Prep time: 10 minutes

Cook time: 20 minutes

Nutritional values (per serving): Calories: 350, Fat: 28g, Protein: 18g, Carbs: 5g

Ingredients:

- 1 pound breakfast sausage, browned and crumbled
- 1/2 cup chopped onion
- 1/2 cup chopped green bell pepper
- 1/2 cup chopped mushrooms
- 1/2 cup chopped zucchini
- Salt and pepper to taste

Instructions:

1. Sauté onion, bell pepper, mushrooms, and zucchini in a skillet until softened.
2. Add sausage and cook until heated through.
3. Season with salt and pepper.
4. Serve warm.

Satisfying Lunches and Dinners

Lemon Herb Roasted Chicken

Prep time: 10 minutes

Cook time: 45-60 minutes

Nutritional values (per serving): Calories: 350, Fat: 25g, Protein: 30g, Carbs: 5g

Ingredients:

- 1 whole chicken (about 3 pounds)
- 2 tablespoons olive oil
- 1 lemon, zested and juiced
- 2 cloves garlic, minced
- 1 tablespoon dried Italian herbs
- Salt and pepper to taste

- **Instructions:**

1. Preheat oven to 400°F (200°C).
2. Pat chicken dry and place in a roasting pan.
3. In a small bowl, combine olive oil, lemon zest, lemon juice, garlic, Italian herbs, salt, and pepper.
4. Rub mixture all over chicken.
5. Roast for 45-60 minutes, or until internal temperature reaches 165°F (75°C).

Creamy Tuscan Garlic Chicken

Prep time: 15 minutes

Cook time: 25 minutes

Nutritional values (per serving): Calories: 450, Fat: 35g, Protein: 30g, Carbs: 5g

Ingredients:

- 2 pounds boneless, skinless chicken breasts, cut into 1-inch pieces
- 2 tablespoons olive oil
- 4 cloves garlic, minced
- 1/2 cup sun-dried tomatoes, packed in oil, chopped
- 1/2 cup heavy cream
- 1/2 cup grated Parmesan cheese
- 1/4 cup chopped fresh basil
- Salt and pepper to taste

- **Instructions:**

1. Heat olive oil in a large skillet over medium-high heat.
2. Add chicken and cook until browned on all sides.
3. Add garlic and sun-dried tomatoes and cook for 1 minute more.
4. Stir in heavy cream and Parmesan cheese. Bring to a simmer and cook until sauce thickens.
5. Stir in basil and season with salt and pepper.

6. Serve over zucchini noodles or cauliflower rice.

Chicken Fajita Bowls

Prep time: 20 minutes

Cook time: 20 minutes

Nutritional values (per serving): Calories: 400, Fat: 25g, Protein: 30g, Carbs: 10g

Ingredients:

- 1 pound boneless, skinless chicken breasts, sliced
- 1 bell pepper (any color), sliced
- 1 onion, sliced
- 2 tablespoons olive oil
- 1 tablespoon chili powder
- 1 teaspoon cumin
- 1/2 teaspoon paprika
- 1/4 teaspoon garlic powder
- Salt and pepper to taste
- Optional toppings: shredded lettuce, diced tomatoes, guacamole, sour cream, salsa

Instructions:

1. In a bowl, combine chicken, bell pepper, onion, olive oil, chili powder, cumin, paprika, garlic powder, salt, and pepper.
2. Heat a large skillet over medium-high heat.

3. Add chicken mixture and cook, stirring occasionally, until chicken is cooked through and vegetables are softened.
4. Serve in bowls with desired toppings.

One-Pan Roasted Chicken with Vegetables

Prep time: 15 minutes

Cook time: 45 minutes

Nutritional values (per serving): Calories: 400, Fat: 28g, Protein: 30g, Carbs: 8g

Ingredients:

- 1 pound boneless, skinless chicken thighs or breasts, cut into 1-inch pieces
- 1 head broccoli, cut into florets
- 1 red onion, cut into wedges
- 1/2 cup cherry tomatoes
- 2 tablespoons olive oil
- 1 teaspoon dried Italian herbs
- Salt and pepper to taste

Instructions:

1. Preheat oven to 400°F (200°C).
2. In a large bowl, combine chicken, broccoli, onion, tomatoes, olive oil, Italian herbs, salt, and pepper. Toss to coat.
3. Spread mixture in a single layer on a baking sheet.

4. Roast for 45 minutes, or until chicken is cooked through and vegetables are tender.

Chicken Salad with Avocado Mayo

Prep time: 15 minutes

Nutritional values (per serving): Calories: 350, Fat: 25g, Protein: 25g, Carbs: 5g

Ingredients:

- 2 cups cooked chicken, shredded
- 1/2 cup chopped celery
- 1/4 cup chopped red onion
- 1/2 avocado, mashed
- 2 tablespoons mayonnaise (optional)
- 1 tablespoon lemon juice
- Salt and pepper to taste

Instructions:

1. Combine all ingredients in a bowl.
2. Mix well and season with salt and pepper.
3. Serve on lettuce leaves, in avocado halves, or with cucumber slices.

Chicken and Broccoli Alfredo (with zoodles)

Prep time: 10 minutes

Cook time: 20 minutes

Nutritional values (per serving): Calories: 450, Fat: 35g, Protein: 30g, Carbs: 8g

Ingredients:

- 1 pound boneless, skinless chicken breasts, cooked and shredded
- 2 medium zucchini, spiralized into zoodles
- 1/2 cup heavy cream
- 1/4 cup grated Parmesan cheese
- 2 cloves garlic, minced
- 1 tablespoon olive oil
- Salt and pepper to taste
- 1 cup broccoli florets

Instructions:

1. Steam or roast broccoli florets until tender.
2. Heat olive oil in a large skillet over medium heat.
3. Add garlic and cook for 30 seconds.
4. Stir in heavy cream and Parmesan cheese. Bring to a simmer and cook until sauce thickens.
5. Add chicken, broccoli, and zoodles to the sauce. Toss to coat.
6. Cook for 5-7 minutes, or until zoodles are tender.
7. Season with salt and pepper and serve.

Chicken Curry with Cauliflower Rice

Prep time: 15 minutes

Cook time: 30 minutes

Nutritional values (per serving): Calories: 400, Fat: 25g, Protein: 35g, Carbs: 10g

Ingredients:

- 1 pound boneless, skinless chicken breasts, cut into 1-inch pieces
- 1 onion, chopped
- 2 cloves garlic, minced
- 1 tablespoon curry powder
- 1 teaspoon ground cumin
- 1/2 teaspoon turmeric
- 1/4 teaspoon cayenne pepper (optional)
- 1 (14 ounce) can coconut milk
- 1 head cauliflower, riced
- Salt and pepper to taste
- Optional toppings: chopped cilantro, chopped peanuts

- **Instructions:**

1. Heat olive oil in a large skillet over medium heat.
2. Add chicken and cook until browned on all sides.
3. Add onion and cook until softened.
4. Stir in garlic, curry powder, cumin, turmeric, and cayenne pepper (if using). Cook for 1 minute more.
5. Pour in coconut milk and bring to a simmer.
6. Add cauliflower rice and cook, stirring occasionally, until tender.

7. Season with salt and pepper.
8. Serve warm with desired toppings.

Coconut Curry Chicken Soup

Prep time: 15 minutes

Cook time: 30 minutes

Nutritional values (per serving): Calories: 380, Fat: 28g, Protein: 25g, Carbs: 7g

Ingredients:

- 1 tablespoon olive oil
- 1 onion, chopped
- 2 cloves garlic, minced
- 1 tablespoon red curry paste
- 1 teaspoon ground ginger
- 1/2 teaspoon turmeric
- 4 cups chicken broth
- 1 (14 ounce) can coconut milk
- 1 pound boneless, skinless chicken breasts, cooked and shredded
- 1/2 cup chopped cauliflower florets
- 1/2 cup chopped broccoli florets
- 1/4 cup chopped fresh cilantro
- Salt and pepper to taste

Instructions:

1. Heat olive oil in a large pot over medium heat.
2. Add onion and cook until softened.

3. Stir in garlic, curry paste, ginger, and turmeric. Cook for 1 minute more.

4. Pour in chicken broth and coconut milk. Bring to a simmer.

5. Add chicken, cauliflower, and broccoli. Simmer for 15 minutes, or until vegetables are tender.

6. Stir in cilantro and season with salt and pepper.

Buffalo Chicken Lettuce Wraps

Prep time: 10 minutes

Cook time: 15 minutes

Nutritional values (per wrap): Calories: 250, Fat: 18g, Protein: 20g, Carbs: 5g

Ingredients:

- 1 pound boneless, skinless chicken breasts, cooked and shredded
- 1/2 cup buffalo sauce (or more to taste)
- 1/4 cup crumbled blue cheese
- 1/4 cup chopped celery
- Lettuce leaves, for wrapping

Instructions:

1. In a bowl, combine shredded chicken, buffalo sauce, blue cheese, and celery.

2. Spoon chicken mixture onto lettuce leaves and wrap.

Creamy Tuscan Chicken Skillet

Prep time: 15 minutes

Cook time: 25 minutes

Nutritional values (per serving): Calories: 450, Fat: 35g, Protein: 30g, Carbs: 5g

Ingredients:

- 2 pounds boneless, skinless chicken breasts, cut into 1-inch pieces
- 2 tablespoons olive oil
- 4 cloves garlic, minced
- 1/2 cup sun-dried tomatoes, packed in oil, chopped
- 1/2 cup heavy cream
- 1/2 cup grated Parmesan cheese
- 1/4 cup chopped fresh spinach
- Salt and pepper to taste

Instructions:

1. Heat olive oil in a large skillet over medium-high heat.

2. Add chicken and cook until browned on all sides.

3. Add garlic and sun-dried tomatoes and cook for 1 minute more.

4. Stir in heavy cream and Parmesan cheese. Bring to a simmer and cook until sauce thickens.

5. Stir in spinach and season with salt and pepper.

6. Serve warm.

Beef and Broccoli Stir-Fry

Prep time: 15 minutes

Cook time: 15 minutes

Nutritional values (per serving): Calories: 350, Fat: 20g, Protein: 30g, Carbs: 10g

Ingredients:

- 1 pound flank steak, thinly sliced
- 2 tablespoons soy sauce (or coconut aminos)
- 1 tablespoon rice vinegar
- 1 teaspoon sesame oil
- 1/2 teaspoon ginger, grated
- 1/4 teaspoon garlic powder
- 1 head broccoli, cut into florets
- 1 tablespoon olive oil
- Salt and pepper to taste

Instructions:

1. In a bowl, combine steak, soy sauce, rice vinegar, sesame oil, ginger, and garlic powder. Marinate for 15 minutes.
2. Steam or roast broccoli florets until tender.
3. Heat olive oil in a large skillet or wok over high heat.
4. Add steak and cook until browned on all sides.
5. Add broccoli and cook, stirring constantly, until heated through.

6. Season with salt and pepper and serve.

Cheeseburger Salad

Prep time: 15 minutes

Cook time: 10 minutes

Nutritional values (per serving): Calories: 450, Fat: 35g, Protein: 25g, Carbs: 5g

Ingredients:

- 1 pound ground beef
- Salt and pepper to taste
- 4 cups mixed greens
- 1/2 cup shredded cheddar cheese
- 1/4 cup diced red onion
- 1/4 cup diced dill pickles
- 1/4 cup sugar-free ketchup
- 1/4 cup sugar-free mustard

Instructions:

1. Cook ground beef in a skillet over medium heat until browned. Season with salt and pepper.
2. In a large bowl, combine mixed greens, cheese, onion, pickles, ketchup, and mustard.
3. Top with cooked ground beef and serve.

Garlic Butter Steak Bites with Mushrooms

Prep time: 10 minutes

Cook time: 15 minutes

Nutritional values (per serving): Calories: 380, Fat: 30g, Protein: 25g, Carbs: 5g

Ingredients:

- 1 pound sirloin steak, cut into 1-inch cubes
- 2 tablespoons butter
- 4 cloves garlic, minced
- 8 ounces mushrooms, sliced
- Salt and pepper to taste
- Chopped fresh parsley, for garnish

Instructions:

1. Melt butter in a large skillet over medium-high heat.
2. Add steak bites and cook until browned on all sides.
3. Add garlic and mushrooms and cook until softened.
4. Season with salt and pepper.
5. Garnish with parsley and serve.

Pork Chops with Roasted Brussels Sprouts

Prep time: 10 minutes

Cook time: 30 minutes

Nutritional values (per serving): Calories: 400, Fat: 28g, Protein: 30g, Carbs: 8g

Ingredients:

- 4 bone-in pork chops
- 1 pound Brussels sprouts, trimmed and halved
- 2 tablespoons olive oil
- 1 teaspoon garlic powder
- 1/2 teaspoon dried thyme
- Salt and pepper to taste

Instructions:

1. Preheat oven to 400°F (200°C).
2. In a bowl, combine Brussels sprouts, olive oil, garlic powder, thyme, salt, and pepper. Toss to coat.
3. Spread Brussels sprouts in a single layer on a baking sheet.
4. Place pork chops on top of Brussels sprouts.
5. Roast for 30 minutes, or until pork chops are cooked through and Brussels sprouts are tender.

Beef Stroganoff (with cauliflower rice or zoodles)

Prep time: 15 minutes

Cook time: 30 minutes

Nutritional values (per serving): Calories: 420, Fat: 32g, Protein: 28g, Carbs: 8g

Ingredients:

- 1 pound sirloin steak, thinly sliced
- 2 tablespoons olive oil
- 1 onion, chopped
- 8 ounces mushrooms, sliced
- 2 cloves garlic, minced
- 1/2 cup beef broth
- 1/2 cup sour cream
- 1/4 cup Dijon mustard
- Salt and pepper to taste
- Cauliflower rice or zoodles, for serving

Instructions:

1. Heat olive oil in a large skillet over medium-high heat.
2. Add steak and cook until browned on all sides. Remove from skillet and set aside.
3. Add onion and mushrooms to the skillet and cook until softened.
4. Stir in garlic and cook for 30 seconds more.
5. Pour in beef broth and bring to a simmer.
6. Stir in sour cream and Dijon mustard.
7. Return steak to the skillet and cook until heated through.
8. Season with salt and pepper.
9. Serve over cauliflower rice or zoodles.

Meatloaf Muffins

Prep time: 15 minutes

Cook time: 25 minutes

Nutritional values (per muffin): Calories: 250, Fat: 20g, Protein: 15g, Carbs: 3g

Ingredients:

- 1 pound ground beef
- 1/2 cup almond flour
- 1 egg
- 1/4 cup chopped onion
- 1/4 cup chopped green bell pepper
- 1/4 cup sugar-free ketchup
- 1 tablespoon Worcestershire sauce
- 1 teaspoon garlic powder
- 1/2 teaspoon dried oregano
- 1/4 teaspoon salt
- 1/4 teaspoon black pepper

Instructions:

1. Preheat oven to 375°F (190°C). Grease a muffin tin.
2. In a large bowl, combine all ingredients and mix well.
3. Divide mixture evenly among muffin cups.
4. Bake for 25 minutes, or until cooked through.

Shepherd's Pie (with cauliflower mash topping)

Prep time: 20 minutes

Cook time: 45 minutes

Nutritional values (per serving): Calories: 480, Fat: 36g, Protein: 30g, Carbs: 10g

Ingredients:

- 1 pound ground lamb or beef
- 1 onion, chopped
- 2 carrots, chopped
- 2 cloves garlic, minced
- 1 cup beef broth
- 1/2 cup frozen peas
- 1 tablespoon tomato paste
- 1 teaspoon Worcestershire sauce
- 1/2 teaspoon dried thyme
- Salt and pepper to taste
- Cauliflower mash topping:
  - 1 head cauliflower, cut into florets
  - 2 tablespoons butter
  - 1/4 cup heavy cream
  - Salt and pepper to taste

Instructions:

1. Preheat oven to 375°F (190°C).
2. In a large skillet over medium heat, brown ground meat.
3. Add onion, carrots, and garlic. Cook until softened.
4. Stir in beef broth, peas, tomato paste, Worcestershire sauce, thyme, salt, and pepper. Bring to a simmer and cook for 15 minutes.
5. Meanwhile, steam or boil cauliflower florets until tender.
6. Mash cauliflower with butter, heavy cream, salt, and pepper.
7. Transfer meat mixture to a baking dish. Top with cauliflower mash.
8. Bake for 20-25 minutes, or until golden brown and bubbly.

Chili Con Carne (no beans)

Prep time: 15 minutes

Cook time: 45 minutes

Nutritional values (per serving): Calories: 400, Fat: 30g, Protein: 25g, Carbs: 5g

Ingredients:

- 1 pound ground beef
- 1 onion, chopped
- 2 cloves garlic, minced
- 1 green bell pepper, chopped
- 1 (14.5 ounce) can diced tomatoes, undrained
- 1 (8 ounce) can tomato sauce
- 2 tablespoons chili powder
- 1 teaspoon cumin
- 1/2 teaspoon paprika
- 1/4 teaspoon cayenne pepper (optional)
- Salt and pepper to taste

Instructions:

1. In a large pot over medium heat, brown ground beef.

2. Add onion, garlic, and bell pepper. Cook until softened.

3. Stir in diced tomatoes, tomato sauce, chili powder, cumin, paprika, cayenne pepper (if using), salt, and pepper.

4. Bring to a boil, then reduce heat and simmer for 30 minutes, or until thickened.

5. Serve warm with desired toppings (e.g., shredded cheese, sour cream, avocado).

Korean Beef Bowls

Prep time: 15 minutes

Cook time: 15 minutes

Nutritional values (per serving): Calories: 420, Fat: 28g, Protein: 30g, Carbs: 10g

Ingredients:

- 1 pound flank steak, thinly sliced
- 2 tablespoons soy sauce (or coconut aminos)
- 1 tablespoon sesame oil
- 1 tablespoon rice vinegar
- 1 tablespoon honey (or sugar-free alternative)
- 1 teaspoon garlic powder
- 1/2 teaspoon ginger, grated
- 1/4 teaspoon red pepper flakes
- 1 tablespoon vegetable oil
- 1/2 head cauliflower, riced
- 1 cucumber, sliced
- 1/2 cup shredded carrots
- Sesame seeds, for garnish

Instructions:

1. In a bowl, combine steak, soy sauce, sesame oil, rice vinegar, honey, garlic powder, ginger, and red pepper flakes. Marinate for 15 minutes.

2. Heat vegetable oil in a large skillet or wok over high heat.

3. Add steak and cook until browned on all sides.

4. In separate pan, cook riced cauliflower according to package directions.

5. Assemble bowls with cauliflower rice, steak, cucumber, carrots, and sesame seeds.

Lamb Chops with Mint Pesto

Prep time: 10 minutes

Cook time: 20 minutes

Nutritional values (per serving): Calories: 450, Fat: 35g, Protein: 25g, Carbs: 5g

Ingredients:

- 4 lamb chops
- Salt and pepper to taste
- Mint pesto:
  - 1 cup fresh mint leaves
  - 1/4 cup olive oil

- 1/4 cup grated Parmesan cheese
- 2 tablespoons pine nuts
- 1 clove garlic, minced
- Salt and pepper to taste

Instructions:

1. Preheat oven to 400°F (200°C).
2. Season lamb chops with salt and pepper.
3. In a food processor, combine all pesto ingredients and pulse until smooth.
4. Place lamb chops on a baking sheet and roast for 15-20 minutes, or until cooked to desired doneness.
5. Top with mint pesto and serve.

Salmon with Lemon-Dill Sauce

Prep time: 5 minutes

Cook time: 15 minutes

Nutritional values (per serving): Calories: 350, Fat: 25g, Protein: 25g, Carbs: 5g

Ingredients:

- 4 (4-ounce) salmon fillets
- 1 tablespoon olive oil
- Salt and pepper to taste
- Lemon-Dill Sauce:
  - 1/4 cup mayonnaise
  - 2 tablespoons lemon juice
  - 2 tablespoons chopped fresh dill
  - 1/4 teaspoon garlic powder

- Salt and pepper to taste

Instructions:

1. Preheat oven to 400°F (200°C).
2. Place salmon fillets on a baking sheet lined with parchment paper.
3. Drizzle with olive oil and season with salt and pepper.
4. Bake for 12-15 minutes, or until cooked through.
5. Meanwhile, whisk together all sauce ingredients in a small bowl.
6. Serve salmon with lemon-dill sauce.

Shrimp Scampi with Zucchini Noodles

Prep time: 10 minutes

Cook time: 15 minutes

Nutritional values (per serving): Calories: 320, Fat: 22g, Protein: 25g, Carbs: 5g

Ingredients:

- 1 pound large shrimp, peeled and deveined
- 2 tablespoons butter
- 4 cloves garlic, minced
- 1/4 cup dry white wine
- 2 medium zucchini, spiralized into zoodles
- 1/4 cup chopped fresh parsley

- Salt and pepper to taste
- Red pepper flakes (optional)

Instructions:

1. Melt butter in a large skillet over medium heat.
2. Add shrimp and cook until pink and opaque. Remove from skillet and set aside.
3. Add garlic to the skillet and cook for 30 seconds.
4. Pour in white wine and bring to a simmer. Cook until reduced by half.
5. Add zoodles and cook until tender.
6. Return shrimp to the skillet and stir in parsley, salt, pepper, and red pepper flakes (if using).
7. Serve warm.

Tuna Salad Stuffed Avocados

Prep time: 10 minutes

Nutritional values (per serving): Calories: 380, Fat: 30g, Protein: 20g, Carbs: 5g

Ingredients:

- 2 ripe avocados, halved and pitted
- 1 (5 ounce) can tuna, drained
- 1/4 cup mayonnaise
- 1/4 cup chopped celery
  - 1/4 cup chopped red onion
- 1 tablespoon lemon juice

- Salt and pepper to taste

Instructions:

1. In a bowl, combine tuna, mayonnaise, celery, red onion, lemon juice, salt, and pepper.
2. Fill avocado halves with tuna salad.

Baked Cod with Lemon and Herbs

Prep time: 5 minutes

Cook time: 15 minutes

Nutritional values (per serving): Calories: 280, Fat: 18g, Protein: 25g, Carbs: 3g

Ingredients:

- 4 (4-ounce) cod fillets
- 1 tablespoon olive oil
- 1 lemon, sliced
- 2 sprigs fresh thyme
- Salt and pepper to taste

Instructions:

1. Preheat oven to 400°F (200°C).
2. Place cod fillets on a baking sheet lined with parchment paper.
3. Drizzle with olive oil and season with salt and pepper.

4. Top each fillet with a lemon slice and a sprig of thyme.

5. Bake for 12-15 minutes, or until cooked through.

Garlic Butter Shrimp

Prep time: 5 minutes

Cook time: 10 minutes

Nutritional values (per serving): Calories: 250, Fat: 18g, Protein: 20g, Carbs: 2g

Ingredients:

- 1 pound large shrimp, peeled and deveined
- 2 tablespoons butter
- 4 cloves garlic, minced
- 1/4 cup chopped fresh parsley
- Salt and pepper to taste
- Red pepper flakes (optional)

Instructions:

1. Melt butter in a large skillet over medium heat.

2. Add shrimp and cook until pink and opaque.

3. Stir in garlic, parsley, salt, pepper, and red pepper flakes (if using).

Pan-Seared Scallops with Cauliflower Risotto

Prep time: 15 minutes

Cook time: 25 minutes

Nutritional values (per serving): Calories: 400, Fat: 28g, Protein: 25g, Carbs: 10g

Ingredients:

- 1 pound sea scallops, patted dry
- 2 tablespoons butter
- 1 onion, chopped
- 2 cloves garlic, minced
- 1 cup cauliflower rice
- 2 cups chicken broth
- 1/4 cup grated Parmesan cheese
- Salt and pepper to taste
- Chopped fresh parsley, for garnish

Instructions:

1. Heat 1 tablespoon butter in a large skillet over medium-high heat.

2. Sear scallops for 2-3 minutes per side, or until golden brown and cooked through. Remove from skillet and set aside.

3. Melt remaining butter in the skillet. Add onion and cook until softened.

4. Stir in garlic and cauliflower rice. Cook for 1 minute more.

5. Pour in chicken broth and bring to a simmer. Cook until cauliflower is tender and liquid is absorbed.

6. Stir in Parmesan cheese, salt, and pepper.

7. Return scallops to the skillet and cook until heated through.

8. Garnish with parsley and serve.

Salmon Patties

Prep time: 15 minutes

Cook time: 15 minutes

Nutritional values (per serving): Calories: 300, Fat: 20g, Protein: 25g, Carbs: 5g

Ingredients:

- 1 (14 ounce) can salmon, drained and flaked
- 1/2 cup almond flour
- 1 egg, beaten
- 1/4 cup chopped onion
- 1/4 cup chopped fresh dill
- 1 tablespoon lemon juice
- Salt and pepper to taste
- 1 tablespoon olive oil

Instructions:

1. In a bowl, combine salmon, almond flour, egg, onion, dill, lemon juice, salt, and pepper. Mix well.

2. Form into patties.

3. Heat olive oil in a skillet over medium heat.

4. Cook patties for 5-7 minutes per side, or until golden brown and cooked through.

Fish Tacos with Cabbage Shells

Prep time: 10 minutes

Cook time: 15 minutes

Nutritional values (per taco): Calories: 280, Fat: 18g, Protein: 20g, Carbs: 5g

Ingredients:

- 1 pound white fish fillets (cod, tilapia, etc.)
- 1 tablespoon taco seasoning
- 1 tablespoon olive oil
- Cabbage leaves, for shells
- Optional toppings: salsa, guacamole, sour cream, shredded cheese

Instructions:

1. Season fish with taco seasoning.
2. Heat olive oil in a skillet over medium heat.
3. Cook fish for 3-5 minutes per side, or until cooked through.
4. Flake fish with a fork.
5. Fill cabbage leaves with fish and desired toppings.

Clam Chowder (no potatoes)

Prep time: 10 minutes

Cook time: 20 minutes

Nutritional values (per serving): Calories: 350, Fat: 25g, Protein: 20g, Carbs: 8g

Ingredients:

- 2 tablespoons butter
- 1 onion, chopped
- 2 cloves garlic, minced
- 1/2 cup chopped celery
- 1/2 cup chopped carrots
- 1/2 cup chopped cauliflower florets
- 4 cups clam juice
- 1 (6.5 ounce) can chopped clams, undrained
- 1/2 cup heavy cream
- Salt and pepper to taste
- Chopped fresh parsley, for garnish

Instructions:

1. Melt butter in a large pot over medium heat.
2. Add onion, garlic, celery, and carrots. Cook until softened.
3. Add cauliflower and cook for 1 minute more.
4. Pour in clam juice and bring to a simmer.
5. Add clams and heavy cream. Heat through, but do not boil.
6. Season with salt and pepper.

7. Garnish with parsley and serve.

One-Pan Baked Fish with Mediterranean Vegetables

Prep time: 15 minutes

Cook time: 25 minutes

Nutritional values (per serving): Calories: 400, Fat: 28g, Protein: 30g, Carbs: 8g

Ingredients:

- 4 (4-ounce) white fish fillets (cod, tilapia, etc.)
- 1 zucchini, sliced
- 1 yellow squash, sliced
- 1 red onion, sliced
- 1/2 cup cherry tomatoes
- 1/4 cup Kalamata olives, pitted
- 2 tablespoons olive oil
- 1 tablespoon lemon juice
- 1 teaspoon dried oregano
- Salt and pepper to taste

Instructions:

1. Preheat oven to 400°F (200°C).
2. In a large bowl, combine vegetables, olive oil, lemon juice, oregano, salt, and pepper. Toss to coat.
3. Spread vegetables in a single layer on a baking sheet.

4. Place fish fillets on top of vegetables.

5. Bake for 20-25 minutes, or until fish is cooked through and vegetables are tender.

Cauliflower Mac and Cheese

Prep time: 15 minutes

Cook time: 30 minutes

Nutritional values (per serving): Calories: 350, Fat: 25g, Protein: 15g, Carbs: 10g

Ingredients:

- 1 head cauliflower, cut into florets
- 2 tablespoons butter
- 2 tablespoons cream cheese
- 1/2 cup heavy cream
- 1/2 cup shredded cheddar cheese
- 1/4 cup grated Parmesan cheese
- Salt and pepper to taste

Instructions:

1. Steam or boil cauliflower florets until tender.

2. While cauliflower is cooking, melt butter in a saucepan over medium heat.

3. Whisk in cream cheese until smooth.

4. Gradually whisk in heavy cream until incorporated.

5. Reduce heat to low and stir in cheddar and Parmesan cheese until melted and smooth.

6. Add cooked cauliflower to the cheese sauce and mash with a potato masher or fork until desired consistency is reached.

7. Season with salt and pepper.

8. Transfer to a baking dish and bake for 10-15 minutes, or until golden brown and bubbly.

Eggplant Parmesan (breaded with almond flour)

Prep time: 20 minutes

Cook time: 45 minutes

Nutritional values (per serving): Calories: 400, Fat: 30g, Protein: 15g, Carbs: 10g

Ingredients:

- 1 large eggplant, sliced into 1/2-inch thick rounds
- 1/2 cup almond flour
- 1/2 teaspoon garlic powder
- 1/4 teaspoon salt
- 1/4 teaspoon black pepper
- 1 egg, beaten
- 1/4 cup olive oil
- 1 cup marinara sauce
- 1/2 cup shredded mozzarella cheese

- 1/4 cup grated Parmesan cheese

Instructions:

1. Preheat oven to 400°F (200°C).

2. In a shallow dish, combine almond flour, garlic powder, salt, and pepper.

3. Dip eggplant slices in beaten egg, then dredge in almond flour mixture.

4. Heat olive oil in a large skillet over medium heat.

5. Cook eggplant slices for 2-3 minutes per side, or until golden brown.

6. Spread a thin layer of marinara sauce in the bottom of a baking dish.

7. Layer eggplant slices, marinara sauce, and mozzarella cheese.

8. Repeat layers, ending with mozzarella cheese.

9. Sprinkle with Parmesan cheese.

10. Bake for 20-25 minutes, or until cheese is melted and bubbly.

Portobello Mushroom Pizzas

Prep time: 10 minutes

Cook time: 20 minutes

Nutritional values (per serving): Calories: 250, Fat: 18g, Protein: 10g, Carbs: 5g

Ingredients:

- 4 large portobello mushrooms, stems removed
- 1/2 cup marinara sauce
- 1/2 cup shredded mozzarella cheese
- Optional toppings: pepperoni, sausage, mushrooms, onions, peppers

Instructions:

1. Preheat oven to 400°F (200°C).
2. Place mushroom caps on a baking sheet lined with parchment paper.
3. Brush with olive oil and season with salt and pepper.
4. Bake for 10 minutes.
5. Remove from oven and top with marinara sauce, cheese, and desired toppings.
6. Bake for another 10 minutes, or until cheese is melted and bubbly.

Zucchini Lasagna

Prep time: 20 minutes

Cook time: 45 minutes

Nutritional values (per serving): Calories: 380, Fat: 28g, Protein: 18g, Carbs: 8g

Ingredients:

- 2 large zucchini, thinly sliced lengthwise
- 1 jar marinara sauce (low-sugar)
- 1 (15 ounce) container ricotta cheese
- 1/2 cup grated Parmesan cheese
- 1 egg
- 1/4 cup chopped fresh basil
- Salt and pepper to taste

Instructions:

1. Preheat oven to 375°F (190°C).

2. In a bowl, combine ricotta cheese, Parmesan cheese, egg, and basil. Season with salt and pepper.

3. Spread a thin layer of marinara sauce in the bottom of a baking dish.

4. Layer zucchini slices, ricotta mixture, and marinara sauce.

5. Repeat layers, ending with marinara sauce.

6. Bake for 40-45 minutes, or until zucchini is tender and bubbly.

Vegetable Frittata

Prep time: 15 minutes

Cook time: 25 minutes

Nutritional values (per serving): Calories: 280, Fat: 20g, Protein: 15g, Carbs: 5g

Ingredients:

- 1 tablespoon olive oil
- 1/2 cup chopped onion
- 1/2 cup chopped green bell pepper
- 1/2 cup chopped mushrooms
- 1 cup chopped broccoli florets
- 6 eggs
- 1/4 cup heavy cream
- 1/4 cup shredded cheddar cheese
- Salt and pepper to taste

Instructions:

1. Preheat oven to 350°F (175°C).

2. Heat olive oil in a large oven-safe skillet over medium heat.

3. Add onion, bell pepper, mushrooms, and broccoli. Cook until softened.

4. Whisk together eggs and heavy cream. Season with salt and pepper.

5. Pour egg mixture over vegetables in the skillet.

6. Sprinkle with cheese.

7. Transfer skillet to oven and bake for 20-25 minutes, or until set.

Cream of Mushroom Soup

Prep time: 10 minutes

Cook time: 25 minutes

Nutritional values (per serving): Calories: 220, Fat: 18g, Protein: 8g, Carbs: 5g

Ingredients:

- 2 tablespoons butter
- 1 onion, chopped
- 8 ounces mushrooms, sliced
- 2 cloves garlic, minced
- 4 cups chicken broth (or vegetable broth)
- 1/2 cup heavy cream
- Salt and pepper to taste
- Chopped fresh parsley, for garnish

Instructions:

1. Melt butter in a large pot over medium heat.

2. Add onion and cook until softened.

3. Add mushrooms and cook until browned.

4. Stir in garlic and cook for 30 seconds more.

5. Pour in chicken broth and bring to a simmer. Cook for 15 minutes.

6. Puree soup with an immersion blender or in a food processor.

7. Return soup to the pot and stir in heavy cream.

8. Season with salt and pepper.

9. Garnish with parsley and serve.

Stuffed Bell Peppers (with cauliflower rice filling)

Prep time: 15 minutes

Cook time: 45 minutes

Nutritional values (per serving): Calories: 350, Fat: 25g, Protein: 15g, Carbs: 10g

Ingredients:

- 4 bell peppers (any color), halved and seeded
- 1 tablespoon olive oil
- 1 onion, chopped
- 1 pound ground beef or turkey
- 1 cup cauliflower rice
- 1 (14.5 ounce) can diced tomatoes, undrained
- 1 teaspoon chili powder
- 1/2 teaspoon cumin
- 1/4 teaspoon salt
- 1/4 teaspoon black pepper
- 1/2 cup shredded cheddar cheese

Instructions:

1. Preheat oven to 375°F (190°C).
2. Brush bell pepper halves with olive oil and place in a baking dish.
3. In a large skillet over medium heat, cook onion and ground meat until browned.
4. Add cauliflower rice, diced tomatoes, chili powder, cumin, salt, and pepper. Cook until heated through.

5. Fill bell pepper halves with meat mixture.

6. Top with cheese.

7. Bake for 25-30 minutes, or until peppers are tender and cheese is melted and bubbly.

Eggplant Rollatini

Prep time: 20 minutes

Cook time: 30 minutes

Nutritional values (per serving): Calories: 380, Fat: 28g, Protein: 15g, Carbs: 8g

Ingredients:

- 1 large eggplant, sliced thinly lengthwise
- 1 (15 ounce) container ricotta cheese
- 1/2 cup grated Parmesan cheese
- 1 egg
- 1/4 cup chopped fresh basil
- Salt and pepper to taste
- 1 jar marinara sauce (low-sugar)
- 1/2 cup shredded mozzarella cheese

Instructions:

1. Preheat oven to 375°F (190°C).

2. Brush eggplant slices with olive oil and grill or broil until tender.

3. In a bowl, combine ricotta cheese, Parmesan cheese, egg, and basil. Season with salt and pepper.

4. Spread a thin layer of ricotta mixture onto each eggplant slice.

5. Roll up eggplant slices and place in a baking dish.

6. Top with marinara sauce and mozzarella cheese.

7. Bake for 20-25 minutes, or until cheese is melted and bubbly.

Spinach and Feta Stuffed Portobello Mushrooms

Prep time: 10 minutes

Cook time: 20 minutes

Nutritional values (per serving): Calories: 200, Fat: 15g, Protein: 10g, Carbs: 5g

Ingredients:

- 4 large portobello mushrooms, stems removed
- 1/2 cup chopped spinach
- 1/4 cup crumbled feta cheese
- 1/4 cup chopped red onion
- 2 tablespoons olive oil
- Salt and pepper to taste

Instructions:

1. Preheat oven to 400°F (200°C).

2. In a bowl, combine spinach, feta cheese, red onion, olive oil, salt, and pepper.

3. Fill mushroom caps with spinach mixture.

4. Bake for 15-20 minutes, or until mushrooms are tender and filling is heated through.

Creamy Broccoli Cheddar Soup (with cauliflower)

Prep time: 10 minutes

Cook time: 25 minutes

Nutritional values (per serving): Calories: 280, Fat: 22g, Protein: 10g, Carbs: 8g

Ingredients:

- 2 tablespoons butter
- 1 onion, chopped
- 1 head cauliflower, cut into florets
- 2 cups broccoli florets
- 4 cups chicken broth (or vegetable broth)
- 1/2 cup heavy cream
- 1/2 cup shredded cheddar cheese
- Salt and pepper to taste

Instructions:

1. Melt butter in a large pot over medium heat.

2. Add onion and cook until softened.

3. Add cauliflower and broccoli. Cook for 5 minutes.

4. Pour in chicken broth and bring to a simmer. Cook until vegetables are tender.

5. Puree soup with an immersion blender or in a food processor.

6. Return soup to the pot and stir in heavy cream and cheddar cheese.

7. Season with salt and pepper.

8. Serve warm.

Snacks and Sides

Avocado Deviled Eggs:

Prep time: 15 minutes

Nutritional values (per egg): Calories: 100, Fat: 9g, Protein: 4g, Carbs: 1g

Ingredients:

- 6 hard-boiled eggs, halved
- 1 ripe avocado, mashed
- 1 tablespoon mayonnaise (optional)
- 1 teaspoon Dijon mustard
- Salt and pepper to taste
- Paprika, for garnish

Instructions:

1. Remove yolks from hard-boiled eggs and place in a bowl.
2. Mash yolks with avocado, mayonnaise (if using), mustard, salt, and pepper.
3. Spoon mixture back into egg whites.
4. Sprinkle with paprika.

Hard-Boiled Eggs:

Prep time: 5 minutes

Cook time: 10-12 minutes

Nutritional values (per egg): Calories: 78, Fat: 5g, Protein: 6g, Carbs: 1g

Ingredients:

- Eggs
- Water

- **Instructions:**

1. Place eggs in a saucepan and cover with cold water.
2. Bring to a boil.
3. Once boiling, turn off heat and cover. Let sit for 10-12 minutes.
4. Drain and peel under cold water.

Cucumber Slices with Cream Cheese:

Prep time: 5 minutes

Nutritional values (per serving): Calories: 100, Fat: 9g, Protein: 2g, Carbs: 2g

Ingredients:

- 1 cucumber, sliced
- 4 ounces cream cheese, softened

Instructions:

1. Spread cream cheese on cucumber slices.

Celery Sticks with Almond Butter:

Prep time: 5 minutes

Nutritional values (per serving): Calories: 190, Fat: 16g, Protein: 7g, Carbs: 4g

Ingredients:

- 4 stalks celery, cut into sticks
- 1/4 cup almond butter

Instructions:

- o Fill celery sticks with almond butter.

Mixed Nuts and Seeds:

Prep time: None

Nutritional values (per 1/4 cup): Calories: 200, Fat: 18g, Protein: 6g, Carbs: 4g

Ingredients:

- 1/4 cup almonds
- 1/4 cup walnuts
- 1/4 cup pumpkin seeds
- 1/4 cup sunflower seeds

Instructions:

1. Combine all ingredients in a bowl.

Berries with Whipped Cream:

Prep time: 5 minutes

Nutritional values (per serving): Calories: 200, Fat: 18g, Protein: 2g, Carbs: 7g

Ingredients:

- 1 cup mixed berries (strawberries, raspberries, blueberries)
- 1/2 cup heavy whipping cream
- 1/4 teaspoon vanilla extract

Instructions:

1. In a small bowl, whip heavy cream and vanilla extract until soft peaks form.
2. Divide berries among bowls and top with whipped cream.

Sugar-Free Jello with Whipped Cream:

Prep time: 5 minutes

Chill time: 4 hours

Nutritional values (per serving): Calories: 100, Fat: 8g, Protein: 1g, Carbs: 2g

Ingredients:

- 1 box sugar-free gelatin
- 1 cup boiling water
- 1 cup cold water
- 1/2 cup heavy whipping cream

- 1/4 teaspoon vanilla extract

Instructions:

1. Dissolve gelatin in boiling water.

2. Stir in cold water and refrigerate for at least 4 hours.

3. In a small bowl, whip heavy cream and vanilla extract until soft peaks form.

4. Top jello with whipped cream.

8. Coconut Chips:

Prep time: None (if using store-bought)

Nutritional values (per serving): Calories: 180, Fat: 17g, Protein: 2g, Carbs: 5g

Ingredients:

- Unsweetened coconut chips

Instructions:

1. Enjoy as a snack straight from the bag.

Kale Chips:

Prep time: 5 minutes

Cook time: 15 minutes

Nutritional values (per serving): Calories: 150, Fat: 12g, Protein: 4g, Carbs: 5g

Ingredients:

- 1 bunch kale, washed and torn into pieces
- 1 tablespoon olive oil
- Salt and pepper to taste

Instructions:

1. Preheat oven to 350°F (175°C).

2. Toss kale with olive oil, salt, and pepper.

3. Spread kale in a single layer on a baking sheet.

4. Bake for 10-15 minutes, or until crispy.

Pork Rinds:

Prep time: None

Nutritional values (per serving): Calories: 150, Fat: 9g, Protein: 17g, Carbs: 0g

Ingredients:

- Plain, unflavored pork rinds

Instructions:

1. Enjoy as a crunchy snack.

Roasted Asparagus:

Prep time: 5 minutes

Cook time: 15 minutes

Nutritional values (per serving): Calories: 50, Fat: 3g, Protein: 3g, Carbs: 2g

Ingredients:

- 1 bunch asparagus, trimmed
- 1 tablespoon olive oil
- Salt and pepper to taste

Instructions:

1. Preheat oven to 400°F (200°C).
2. Toss asparagus with olive oil, salt, and pepper.
3. Spread in a single layer on a baking sheet.
4. Roast for 12-15 minutes, or until tender.

Sautéed Spinach with Garlic:

Prep time: 5 minutes

Cook time: 5 minutes

Nutritional values (per serving): Calories: 80, Fat: 6g, Protein: 3g, Carbs: 2g

Ingredients:

- 1 tablespoon olive oil
- 2 cloves garlic, minced
- 4 cups fresh spinach
- Salt and pepper to taste

Instructions:

1. Heat olive oil in a skillet over medium heat.
2. Add garlic and cook for 30 seconds.
3. Add spinach and cook until wilted.
4. Season with salt and pepper.

Roasted Brussels Sprouts with Bacon:

Prep time: 10 minutes

Cook time: 25 minutes

Nutritional values (per serving): Calories: 180, Fat: 15g, Protein: 6g, Carbs: 5g

Ingredients:

- 1 pound Brussels sprouts, trimmed and halved
- 4 slices bacon, diced
- 1 tablespoon olive oil
- Salt and pepper to taste

Instructions:

1. Preheat oven to 400°F (200°C).
2. Cook bacon in a skillet until crisp. Remove and set aside.
3. Toss Brussels sprouts with olive oil, salt, and pepper.
4. Spread in a single layer on a baking sheet.
5. Roast for 20 minutes.
6. Add bacon to the baking sheet and roast for 5 more minutes.

Garlic Parmesan Roasted Cauliflower:

Prep time: 10 minutes

Cook time: 25 minutes

Nutritional values (per serving): Calories: 120, Fat: 9g, Protein: 4g, Carbs: 5g

Ingredients:

- 1 head cauliflower, cut into florets
- 2 tablespoons olive oil
- 2 cloves garlic, minced
- 1/4 cup grated Parmesan cheese
- Salt and pepper to taste

Instructions:

1. Preheat oven to 400°F (200°C).
2. Toss cauliflower florets with olive oil, garlic, salt, and pepper.
3. Spread in a single layer on a baking sheet.
4. Roast for 20 minutes.
5. Sprinkle with Parmesan cheese and roast for 5 more minutes.

Creamy Spinach:

Prep time: 5 minutes

Cook time: 10 minutes

Nutritional values (per serving): Calories: 150, Fat: 12g, Protein: 4g, Carbs: 3g

Ingredients:

- 1 tablespoon butter
- 2 cloves garlic, minced
- 4 cups fresh spinach
- 1/4 cup heavy cream
- Salt and pepper to taste
- Pinch of nutmeg

Instructions:

1. Melt butter in a skillet over medium heat.
2. Add garlic and cook for 30 seconds.
3. Add spinach and cook until wilted.
4. Stir in heavy cream and nutmeg. Season with salt and pepper.
5. Cook until heated through.

Steamed Broccoli with Lemon Butter:

Prep time: 5 minutes

Cook time: 5 minutes

Nutritional values (per serving): Calories: 100, Fat: 8g, Protein: 3g, Carbs: 4g

Ingredients:

- 1 head broccoli, cut into florets

- 2 tablespoons butter
- 1 tablespoon lemon juice
- Salt and pepper to taste

Instructions:

1. Steam broccoli florets until tender.
2. In a small saucepan, melt butter over low heat.
3. Stir in lemon juice, salt, and pepper.
4. Drizzle lemon butter over broccoli and serve.

Cucumber and Avocado Salad:

Prep time: 10 minutes

Nutritional values (per serving): Calories: 200, Fat: 18g, Protein: 2g, Carbs: 4g

Ingredients:

- 1 cucumber, diced
- 1 avocado, diced
- 1/4 cup chopped red onion
- 2 tablespoons olive oil
- 1 tablespoon red wine vinegar
- Salt and pepper to taste
- Chopped fresh dill, for garnish

Instructions:

1. In a bowl, combine cucumber, avocado, red onion, olive oil, red wine vinegar, salt, and pepper.
2. Toss gently to combine.
3. Garnish with dill and serve.

Zucchini Noodles:

Prep time: 10 minutes

Nutritional values (per serving): Calories: 50, Fat: 0g, Protein: 1g, Carbs: 8g

Ingredients:

- 2 medium zucchini, spiralized into noodles

Instructions:

1. Use a spiralizer or vegetable peeler to create zucchini noodles.
2. Serve raw or sautéed in olive oil.

Cauliflower Rice:

Prep time: 10 minutes

Nutritional values (per serving): Calories: 25, Fat: 0g, Protein: 2g, Carbs: 5g

Ingredients:

- 1 head cauliflower, cut into florets

Instructions:

1. Grate cauliflower florets using a box grater or food processor.
2. Serve raw or sautéed in olive oil.

Roasted Radishes with Herbs:

Prep time: 10 minutes

Cook time: 20 minutes

Nutritional values (per serving): Calories: 80, Fat: 6g, Protein: 1g, Carbs: 4g

Ingredients:

- 1 bunch radishes, trimmed and quartered
- 1 tablespoon olive oil
- 1/2 teaspoon dried thyme
- 1/4 teaspoon dried rosemary
- Salt and pepper to taste

Instructions:

1. Preheat oven to 400°F (200°C).
2. Toss radishes with olive oil, thyme, rosemary, salt, and pepper.
3. Spread in a single layer on a baking sheet.
4. Roast for 20 minutes, or until tender and slightly browned.

Desserts and Treats

Avocado Chocolate Mousse:

Prep time: 10 minutes

Nutritional values (per serving): Calories: 250, Fat: 20g, Protein: 5g, Carbs: 8g

Ingredients:

- 1 ripe avocado
- 1/4 cup unsweetened cocoa powder
- 1/4 cup sweetener (e.g., stevia, erythritol)
- 1/4 cup unsweetened almond milk
- 1 teaspoon vanilla extract

Instructions:

1. Combine all ingredients in a food processor or blender.
2. Blend until smooth and creamy.
3. Chill for at least 30 minutes before serving.

Coconut Cream Pie:

Prep time: 20 minutes

Chill time: 4 hours

Nutritional values (per serving): Calories: 350, Fat: 30g, Protein: 5g, Carbs: 10g

Ingredients:

- 1 cup almond flour
- 1/4 cup coconut oil, melted
- 1 egg
- 1/4 teaspoon salt
- 1 (14 ounce) can full-fat coconut milk
- 1/2 cup sweetener (e.g., stevia, erythritol)
- 1/4 cup arrowroot powder or cornstarch
- 2 teaspoons vanilla extract

Instructions:

1. Preheat oven to 350°F (175°C).
2. Combine almond flour, coconut oil, egg, and salt in a bowl. Press into a pie plate.
3. Bake for 10-12 minutes, or until golden brown.
4. In a saucepan, combine coconut milk, sweetener, and arrowroot powder/cornstarch.
5. Cook over medium heat, stirring constantly, until thickened.
6. Remove from heat and stir in vanilla extract.
7. Pour filling into the baked crust and refrigerate for at least 4 hours.

Lemon Chia Seed Pudding:

Prep time: 5 minutes

Chill time: 2 hours

Nutritional values (per serving): Calories: 200, Fat: 15g, Protein: 4g, Carbs: 8g

Ingredients:

- 1/4 cup chia seeds
- 1 cup unsweetened almond milk
- 2 tablespoons lemon juice
- 1 tablespoon sweetener (e.g., stevia, erythritol)
- 1/4 teaspoon vanilla extract
- Zest of 1 lemon, for garnish

Instructions:

- Combine all ingredients in a jar or bowl.
- Stir well and refrigerate for at least 2 hours.
- Garnish with lemon zest before serving.

Keto Cheesecake Fat Bombs:

Prep time: 15 minutes

Freeze time: 1 hour

Nutritional values (per bomb): Calories: 150, Fat: 14g, Protein: 3g, Carbs: 2g

Ingredients:

- 8 ounces cream cheese, softened
- 1/4 cup sweetener (e.g., stevia, erythritol)
- 1 teaspoon vanilla extract
- 1/4 cup melted coconut oil

Instructions:

1. Beat cream cheese, sweetener, and vanilla extract until smooth.
2. Gradually beat in melted coconut oil.
3. Spoon mixture into silicone molds or mini muffin tins.
4. Freeze for at least 1 hour, or until firm.

Berries with Whipped Cream and Mascarpone:

Prep time: 5 minutes

Nutritional values (per serving): Calories: 250, Fat: 20g, Protein: 4g, Carbs: 8g

Ingredients:

- 1 cup mixed berries
- 1/4 cup mascarpone cheese
- 1/4 cup heavy whipping cream
- 1/4 teaspoon vanilla extract

Instructions:

1. In a small bowl, whip mascarpone cheese, heavy cream, and vanilla extract until soft peaks form.
2. Divide berries among bowls and top with mascarpone cream.

Raspberry Chia Jam:

Prep time: 5 minutes

Chill time: 2 hours

Nutritional values (per serving): Calories: 60, Fat: 3g, Protein: 1g, Carbs: 7g

Ingredients:

- 1 cup fresh or frozen raspberries
- 1 tablespoon chia seeds
- 1-2 teaspoons sweetener (e.g., stevia, erythritol) to taste
- 1 tablespoon lemon juice (optional)

Instructions:

1. In a small saucepan, combine raspberries and sweetener.

2. Heat over medium heat, mashing berries with a fork until softened.

3. Remove from heat and stir in chia seeds and lemon juice (if using).

4. Let cool for 5 minutes, then transfer to a jar and refrigerate for at least 2 hours.

No-Bake Peanut Butter Cookies:

Prep time: 15 minutes

Chill time: 30 minutes

Nutritional values (per cookie): Calories: 150, Fat: 12g, Protein: 5g, Carbs: 4g

Ingredients:

- 1 cup natural peanut butter
- 1/4 cup coconut oil, melted
- 1/4 cup sweetener (e.g., stevia, erythritol)
- 1/4 cup unsweetened shredded coconut
- 1/4 cup chopped nuts (optional)

Instructions:

1. In a bowl, combine all ingredients and mix well.

2. Roll into small balls and place on a baking sheet lined with parchment paper.

3. Chill for at least 30 minutes before serving.

Chocolate Avocado Pudding:

Prep time: 10 minutes

Nutritional values (per serving): Calories: 200, Fat: 16g, Protein: 3g, Carbs: 8g

Ingredients:

- 1 ripe avocado
- 1/4 cup unsweetened cocoa powder
- 1/4 cup sweetener (e.g., stevia, erythritol)
- 1/4 cup unsweetened almond milk
- 1 teaspoon vanilla extract

Instructions:

1. Combine all ingredients in a food processor or blender.

2. Blend until smooth and creamy.

3. Serve chilled.

Keto Brownies:

Prep time: 15 minutes

Cook time: 25 minutes

Nutritional values (per serving): Calories: 180, Fat: 16g, Protein: 4g, Carbs: 5g

Ingredients:

- 1/2 cup almond flour
- 1/4 cup coconut flour
- 1/2 cup unsweetened cocoa powder
- 1/4 teaspoon baking powder
- 1/4 teaspoon salt
- 1/2 cup melted butter or coconut oil
- 2 eggs
- 1/2 cup sweetener (e.g., stevia, erythritol)
- 1 teaspoon vanilla extract
- 1/4 cup chopped nuts (optional)

Instructions:

1. Preheat oven to 350°F (175°C). Grease an 8x8 inch baking pan.

2. In a bowl, combine all dry ingredients.

3. In a separate bowl, whisk together melted butter, eggs, sweetener, and vanilla extract.

4. Pour wet ingredients into dry ingredients and mix until just combined.

5. Fold in chopped nuts (if using).

6. Spread batter into prepared pan.

7. Bake for 20-25 minutes, or until a toothpick inserted into the center comes out clean.

Coconut Flour Cupcakes:

Prep time: 15 minutes

Cook time: 20 minutes

Nutritional values (per cupcake): Calories: 160, Fat: 14g, Protein: 4g, Carbs: 4g

Ingredients:

- 1 cup coconut flour
- 1/2 teaspoon baking powder
- 1/4 teaspoon salt
- 1/4 cup melted coconut oil or butter
- 1/4 cup unsweetened almond milk
- 2 eggs
- 1 teaspoon vanilla extract
- 1/4 cup sweetener (e.g., stevia, erythritol)
- Optional frosting: whipped cream cheese, berries

Instructions:

1. Preheat oven to 350°F (175°C). Line a muffin tin with paper liners.

2. In a bowl, combine coconut flour, baking powder, and salt.

3. In a separate bowl, whisk together melted coconut oil, almond milk, eggs, vanilla extract, and sweetener.

4. Pour wet ingredients into dry ingredients and mix until just combined. Do not overmix.

5. Divide batter evenly among muffin cups.

6. Bake for 18-20 minutes, or until golden brown and a toothpick inserted into the center comes out clean.

7. Frost with whipped cream cheese and berries (optional).

Strawberry Shortcake (with almond flour biscuits):

Prep time: 20 minutes

Cook time: 15 minutes

Nutritional values (per serving): Calories: 280, Fat: 20g, Protein: 5g, Carbs: 12g

Ingredients:

- Biscuits:
  - 1 cup almond flour
  - 1 tablespoon coconut flour
  - 1 teaspoon baking powder
  - 1/4 teaspoon salt
  - 1/4 cup cold butter, cubed
  - 1/4 cup unsweetened almond milk

- Filling:
  - 2 cups sliced strawberries
  - 1/4 cup sweetener (e.g., stevia, erythritol)
  - 1/4 cup heavy whipping cream, whipped

- **Instructions:**

1. Preheat oven to 400°F (200°C).

2. In a bowl, combine almond flour, coconut flour, baking powder, and salt.

3. Cut in butter until mixture resembles coarse crumbs.

4. Stir in almond milk until a dough forms.

5. Drop dough by spoonfuls onto a baking sheet lined with parchment paper.

6. Bake for 12-15 minutes, or until golden brown.

7. While biscuits are baking, toss strawberries with sweetener.

8. To assemble, split biscuits in half and layer with strawberries and whipped cream.

Lemon Bars (with almond flour crust):

Prep time: 15 minutes

Cook time: 30 minutes

Nutritional values (per serving): Calories: 220, Fat: 18g, Protein: 4g, Carbs: 8g

Ingredients:

- Crust:
    - 1 cup almond flour
    - 1/4 cup melted butter
    - 1/4 cup sweetener (e.g., stevia, erythritol)
    - 1/4 teaspoon salt
- Filling:
    - 4 eggs
    - 1 cup lemon juice
    - 1/2 cup sweetener (e.g., stevia, erythritol)
    - 1/4 cup almond flour
    - Zest of 1 lemon

Instructions:

1. Preheat oven to 350°F (175°C).
2. Press crust ingredients into the bottom of an 8x8 inch baking pan.
3. Bake for 10-12 minutes, or until golden brown.
4. Whisk together filling ingredients in a bowl.
5. Pour filling over the baked crust.
6. Bake for 20-25 minutes, or until filling is set.
7. Cool completely before cutting into bars.

Chocolate Chip Cookies (with almond and coconut flour):

Prep time: 15 minutes

Cook time: 12 minutes

Nutritional values (per cookie): Calories: 100, Fat: 9g, Protein: 2g, Carbs: 3g

Ingredients:

- 1 cup almond flour
- 1/4 cup coconut flour
- 1/4 teaspoon baking soda
- 1/4 teaspoon salt
- 1/2 cup softened butter
- 1/4 cup sweetener (e.g., stevia, erythritol)
- 1 egg
- 1 teaspoon vanilla extract
- 1/2 cup sugar-free chocolate chips

Instructions:

1. Preheat oven to 350°F (175°C).
2. In a bowl, combine almond flour, coconut flour, baking soda, and salt.
3. In a separate bowl, cream together butter and sweetener.
4. Beat in egg and vanilla extract.
5. Gradually add dry ingredients to wet ingredients and mix until just combined.
6. Fold in chocolate chips.
7. Drop dough by spoonfuls onto a baking sheet lined with parchment paper.
8. Bake for 10-12 minutes, or until edges are golden brown.

Coffee Ice Cream (with coconut milk):

- **Prep time:** 10 minutes
- **Freeze time:** 4 hours
- **Nutritional values (per serving):** Calories: 150, Fat: 12g, Protein: 1g, Carbs: 4g
- **Ingredients:**
  - 1 (14 ounce) can full-fat coconut milk
  - 1/4 cup sweetener (e.g., stevia, erythritol)
  - 2 tablespoons instant coffee granules
  - 1 teaspoon vanilla extract

- **Instructions:**

1. In a saucepan, combine coconut milk and sweetener.
2. Heat over medium heat, stirring constantly, until sweetener is dissolved.
3. Remove from heat and stir in instant coffee and vanilla extract.
4. Pour mixture into a freezer-safe container and freeze for at least 4 hours, or until solid.

Keto Mug Cake:

Prep time: 5 minutes

Cook time: 1 minute (microwave)

Nutritional values (per cake): Calories: 200, Fat: 18g, Protein: 5g, Carbs: 5g

Ingredients:

- 1 egg
- 1 tablespoon almond butter
- 1 tablespoon coconut oil, melted
- 1 tablespoon sweetener (e.g., stevia, erythritol)
- 1 tablespoon cocoa powder
- 1/4 teaspoon baking powder

- Pinch of salt

Instructions:

1. In a microwave-safe mug, whisk together all ingredients until smooth.

2. Microwave on high for 1 minute, or until cooked through.

3. Top with whipped cream or berries (optional).

Berry Cobbler (with almond flour topping):

Prep time: 15 minutes

Cook time: 30 minutes

Nutritional values (per serving): Calories: 250, Fat: 18g, Protein: 4g, Carbs: 10g

Ingredients:

- Filling:
  - 4 cups mixed berries (strawberries, raspberries, blueberries)
  - 1/4 cup sweetener (e.g., stevia, erythritol)
  - 1 tablespoon lemon juice
- Topping:
  - 1 cup almond flour
  - 1/4 cup melted butter
  - 1/4 cup sweetener (e.g., stevia, erythritol)
  - 1/2 teaspoon cinnamon
  - Pinch of salt

- **Instructions:**

1. Preheat oven to 375°F (190°C).

2. In a bowl, toss berries with sweetener and lemon juice.

3. Spread berries in a baking dish.

4. In a separate bowl, combine almond flour, melted butter, sweetener, cinnamon, and salt.

5. Crumble topping over berries.

6. Bake for 25-30 minutes, or until topping is golden brown and berries are bubbly.

Chocolate Coconut Fat Bombs:

Prep time: 10 minutes

Chill time: 30 minutes

Nutritional values (per bomb): Calories: 180, Fat: 16g, Protein: 2g, Carbs: 3g

Ingredients:

- 1/2 cup coconut oil, melted
- 1/4 cup unsweetened cocoa powder

- 1/4 cup sweetener (e.g., stevia, erythritol)

- 1/4 cup unsweetened shredded coconut

Instructions:

1. In a bowl, combine all ingredients and mix well.

2. Spoon mixture into silicone molds or mini muffin tins.

3. Chill for at least 30 minutes, or until firm.

Keto Ice Cream Sandwiches:

Prep time: 15 minutes

Freeze time: 4 hours

Nutritional values (per sandwich): Calories: 250, Fat: 20g, Protein: 4g, Carbs: 5g

Ingredients:

- 1 recipe keto chocolate chip cookies
- 1 recipe coffee ice cream

Instructions:

- Once cookies are cool, sandwich a scoop of coffee ice cream between two cookies.
- Freeze for at least 1 hour before serving.

Peanut Butter Fudge:

Prep time: 10 minutes

Chill time: 2 hours

Nutritional values (per serving): Calories: 200, Fat: 18g, Protein: 5g, Carbs: 4g

Ingredients:

- 1 cup natural peanut butter
- 1/4 cup coconut oil, melted
- 1/4 cup sweetener (e.g., stevia, erythritol)
- 1/4 cup unsweetened cocoa powder
- 1 teaspoon vanilla extract

Instructions:

1. Line an 8x8 inch pan with parchment paper.

2. In a saucepan over low heat, combine peanut butter, coconut oil, and sweetener. Stir until melted and smooth.

3. Remove from heat and stir in cocoa powder and vanilla extract.

4. Pour mixture into prepared pan and smooth the top.

5. Refrigerate for at least 2 hours, or until firm.

6. Cut into squares and serve.

Whipped Coconut Cream with Berries:

Prep time: 5 minutes

Chill time: 4 hours

Nutritional values (per serving): Calories: 150, Fat: 14g, Protein: 1g, Carbs: 3g

Ingredients:

- 1 (14 ounce) can full-fat coconut milk, chilled
- 1/4 teaspoon vanilla extract
- 1 cup mixed berries

Instructions:

1. Chill coconut milk for at least 4 hours.

2. Scoop out the solidified cream from the top of the can, leaving the liquid behind.

3. Whip coconut cream with vanilla extract until soft peaks form.

4. Serve with berries.

Smoothie recipes

Green Machine:

Prep time: 5 minutes

Nutritional values (per serving): Calories: 250, Fat: 18g, Protein: 8g, Carbs: 7g

Ingredients:

- 1 cup spinach
- 1/2 cup kale
- 1/2 avocado
- 1/2 cucumber
- 1 cup unsweetened almond milk
- 1 tablespoon lemon juice
- 1/2 inch piece ginger (optional)

Instructions:

1. Combine all ingredients in a blender.
2. Blend until smooth and creamy.

Berry Blast:

Prep time: 5 minutes

Nutritional values (per serving): Calories: 300, Fat: 22g, Protein: 7g, Carbs: 8g

Ingredients:

- 1 cup mixed berries (raspberries, blueberries, strawberries)
- 1/2 avocado
- 1 cup unsweetened almond milk
- 1 tablespoon coconut oil
- 1 tablespoon chia seeds
- **Instructions:**

1. Combine all ingredients in a blender.
2. Blend until smooth and creamy.

Creamy Avocado:

Prep time: 5 minutes

Nutritional values (per serving): Calories: 350, Fat: 30g, Protein: 5g, Carbs: 8g

Ingredients:

- 1 avocado
- 1 cup coconut milk
- 1/2 cup spinach
- 1 tablespoon lime juice
- 1/2 inch piece ginger
- 1/4 teaspoon turmeric

- **Instructions:**

1. Combine all ingredients in a blender.
2. Blend until smooth and creamy.

Nutty Delight:

Prep time: 5 minutes

Nutritional values (per serving): Calories: 400, Fat: 32g, Protein: 15g, Carbs: 8g

Ingredients:

- 2 tablespoons almond butter
- 1 cup unsweetened almond milk
- 1/2 cup spinach
- 1 scoop protein powder
- 1/2 teaspoon cinnamon
- 1 tablespoon chia seeds

Instructions:

1. Combine all ingredients in a blender.
2. Blend until smooth and creamy.

Tropical Escape:

Prep time: 5 minutes

Nutritional values (per serving): Calories: 300, Fat: 20g, Protein: 4g, Carbs: 12g

Ingredients:

- 1 cup coconut milk
- 1/2 cup mango (frozen or fresh)
- 1/4 cup pineapple (frozen or fresh)
- 1/2 cup spinach
- 1 tablespoon lime juice
- A few mint leaves

Instructions:

1. Combine all ingredients in a blender.
2. Blend until smooth and creamy.

Ginger Zing:

Prep time: 5 minutes

Nutritional values (per serving): Calories: 150, Fat: 8g, Protein: 3g, Carbs: 8g

Ingredients:

- 1 cup unsweetened almond milk
- 1 inch piece ginger
- 1/2 teaspoon turmeric
- 1 tablespoon lemon juice
- 1/2 cucumber
- 1 cup spinach
- A few mint leaves

Instructions:

1. Combine all ingredients in a blender.
2. Blend until smooth and creamy.

Matcha Magic:

Prep time: 5 minutes

Nutritional values (per serving): Calories: 250, Fat: 18g, Protein: 5g, Carbs: 7g

Ingredients:

- 1 teaspoon matcha powder
- 1 cup unsweetened almond milk
- 1/2 avocado
- 1 cup spinach
- Stevia to taste (optional)

Instructions:

1. Combine all ingredients in a blender.
2. Blend until smooth and creamy.

Chocolate Avocado:

Prep time: 5 minutes

Nutritional values (per serving): Calories: 350, Fat: 28g, Protein: 10g, Carbs: 8g

Ingredients:

- 1 avocado
- 1/4 cup unsweetened cocoa powder

- 1 cup unsweetened almond milk
- 1 teaspoon vanilla extract
- 1 scoop protein powder (optional)
- **Instructions:**

1. Combine all ingredients in a blender.
2. Blend until smooth and creamy.

Pumpkin Spice:

Prep time: 5 minutes

Nutritional values (per serving): Calories: 300, Fat: 25g, Protein: 5g, Carbs: 7g

Ingredients:

- 1/2 cup canned pumpkin puree (unsweetened)
- 1 cup unsweetened almond milk
- 1/2 teaspoon pumpkin pie spice
- 1/2 inch piece ginger
- A few pecans

Instructions:

1. Combine all ingredients in a blender.
2. Blend until smooth and creamy.

Carrot Cake:

Prep time: 5 minutes

Nutritional values (per serving): Calories: 320, Fat: 24g, Protein: 6g, Carbs: 10g

Ingredients:

- 1 medium carrot, roughly chopped

- 1 cup unsweetened almond milk

- 1/2 teaspoon cinnamon

- 1/2 inch piece ginger

- A few walnuts

- 1/4 cup pineapple chunks (optional)

Instructions:

1. Combine all ingredients in a blender.

2. Blend until smooth and creamy.

Chapter 5: Nutritional Supplements for Cancer Patients on Keto

Now, let's talk about something that often gets overlooked in the keto conversation: supplements. While a well-formulated ketogenic diet can provide many of the nutrients you need, cancer and its treatments can put extra stress on your body, making it even more important to ensure you're getting adequate amounts of essential vitamins and minerals.

Think of supplements as your insurance policy. They're not meant to replace a healthy diet, but they can fill in the gaps and provide an extra layer of support, especially when your body is going through a tough time.

Essential Vitamins and Minerals

Think of essential vitamins and minerals as the spark plugs that keep your body's engine running smoothly. Just like a car needs the right mix of fuel and air to function properly, your body relies on these nutrients for everything from energy production to immune function to cell repair.

When you're battling cancer, your body's demand for these essential nutrients can increase. Additionally, certain cancer treatments can interfere with your body's ability to absorb or utilize certain vitamins and minerals. That's why it's crucial to make sure you're getting enough of these key players to support your health and well-being during this challenging time.

Here are some of the essential vitamins and minerals that deserve your attention:

- **Vitamin D:** This isn't just any vitamin; it's practically a superhero! Vitamin D is involved in immune function, bone health, and even mood regulation. Unfortunately, many people, especially those dealing with cancer, are deficient in this crucial nutrient. If you can't get enough sunshine (the best source of vitamin D), consider talking to your doctor about a supplement.

- **B Vitamins:** These guys are like the pit crew of your body, working together to keep your energy levels up and your nerves firing smoothly. Cancer and its treatments can deplete these essential vitamins, so supplementation may be necessary to keep you feeling your best.

- **Zinc:** Think of zinc as the construction worker of your body. It's involved in building and repairing tissues, as well as supporting immune function. Cancer patients often have low zinc levels, so a supplement might be recommended to give your body the building blocks it needs.

- **Magnesium:** This mighty mineral plays a role in hundreds of bodily processes, including energy production, muscle function, and even sleep regulation. Cancer and its treatments can mess with your magnesium levels, so a supplement can help restore balance and promote relaxation.

- **Selenium:** This trace mineral is a potent antioxidant, meaning it helps protect your cells from damage. It also plays a role in immune function and may help reduce the side effects of cancer treatment.

These are just a few of the key vitamins and minerals that are important for cancer patients.

Think of it as a personalized vitamin and mineral tune-up for your body. By ensuring you have adequate levels of these essential nutrients, you're giving yourself the best possible chance to fight back against cancer and thrive throughout your treatment journey

By incorporating the right supplements into your ketogenic lifestyle, you can optimize your nutrient intake, support your body's healing processes, and thrive during cancer treatment. Remember, it's all about finding what works best for you and tailoring your approach to your individual needs.

Supplements for Immune Support

Think of your immune system as your body's defense force, battling against unwanted invaders like infections and illnesses. Now, while a healthy keto diet provides a strong foundation for immune function, cancer and its treatments can weaken these defenses. That's where immune-boosting supplements come in, acting as reinforcements to help your body fight back.

These supplements aren't meant to replace a healthy diet or medical treatment, but they can offer an extra layer of protection and support during this challenging time. They work by providing essential nutrients that your body may be lacking or by enhancing the activity of your immune cells.

Here are some key supplements that have shown promise in supporting immune function in cancer patients:

- **Vitamin C:** This powerful antioxidant helps protect cells from damage and supports various immune cells. Some studies suggest it may even help reduce the side effects of cancer treatment. Look for liposomal vitamin C, which is easier on the stomach and better absorbed by the body.

- **Zinc:** This mineral is crucial for the development and function of immune cells. It's often deficient in cancer patients and may be depleted further by chemotherapy. Zinc supplements can help replenish your levels and support your immune system.

- **Vitamin D:** This sunshine vitamin plays a vital role in regulating immune responses. Many cancer patients are deficient in vitamin D, and research suggests that supplementation may help reduce the risk of infections.

- **Selenium:** This trace mineral is a powerful antioxidant that helps protect cells from damage. It also plays a role in immune function and may help reduce the side effects of radiation therapy.

- **Medicinal Mushrooms:** Certain mushrooms, like reishi, shiitake, and maitake, have been used in traditional medicine for centuries for their immune-boosting properties. They contain compounds that can enhance the activity of immune cells and promote overall health.

While supplements can be a helpful tool, they shouldn't be seen as a magic bullet. The most important thing is to focus on a healthy, balanced diet that provides your body with the nutrients it needs to thrive. Supplements can simply be an added layer of support, helping to strengthen your immune system and promote overall well-being.

More tips for choosing supplements:

- **Look for high-quality brands:** Choose brands that are reputable and third-party tested for purity and potency.

- **Start with small doses:** Gradually increase your dosage as needed and tolerated.

- **Take supplements with food:** This can help improve absorption and minimize any digestive upset.

- **Don't self-medicate:** Always talk to your doctor before starting any new supplement, especially if you're taking prescription medications.

Addressing Nutrient Deficiencies: A Deeper Look

The ketogenic diet, while incredibly beneficial, isn't a one-size-fits-all solution. While it's rich in healthy fats and moderate in protein, certain nutrients can sometimes fall through the cracks. Cancer and its treatments can further exacerbate these deficiencies, making it crucial to identify and address any potential gaps in your nutritional intake.

Think of it like tending to a garden. Even with the best soil and sunlight, certain plants may need a little extra attention to flourish. Similarly, your body may require additional support to ensure optimal health during cancer treatment.

Here's where we roll up our sleeves and take a closer look at potential deficiencies:

Electrolytes: Sodium, potassium, and magnesium are essential minerals that help maintain fluid balance, nerve function, and muscle contractions. The initial transition to keto can cause you to lose these electrolytes more rapidly, leading to symptoms like fatigue, headaches, and muscle cramps.

How to address it: Don't be afraid to salt your food! You can also incorporate bone broth, which is naturally rich in electrolytes, and consider electrolyte supplements if needed.

Fiber: While the keto diet naturally limits high-fiber foods like grains and legumes, it's important to include fiber-rich vegetables like broccoli, cauliflower, and leafy greens. Fiber supports gut health, aids digestion, and can help prevent constipation, a common side effect of cancer treatment.

How to address it: Make non-starchy vegetables a staple in your meals and snacks. You can also try adding a tablespoon of ground flaxseed or chia seeds to your smoothies or yogurt for an extra fiber boost.

Certain Vitamins and Minerals: While keto is naturally rich in some nutrients, like vitamin A and E, it may fall short on others. Vitamin C, for example, is abundant in fruits, which are limited on keto. Similarly, B vitamins, zinc, and selenium may need a closer look.

How to address it: Focus on incorporating keto-friendly sources of these nutrients into your diet. For example, bell peppers, broccoli, and Brussels sprouts are good sources of vitamin C, while meat, fish, and eggs provide B vitamins and zinc. If you're struggling to meet your needs through food alone, talk to your doctor about targeted supplementation.

It's important to note that nutrient deficiencies can vary from person to person, and their symptoms may be subtle or easily overlooked. If you experience unexplained fatigue, muscle weakness, changes in mood or sleep patterns, or any other unusual symptoms, it's worth talking to your doctor to rule out any potential deficiencies.

This is a journey of self-discovery and personalized care. By paying attention to your body's signals and making informed choices about your nutrition, you can ensure that your body has everything it needs to fight cancer and thrive.

Chapter 6: Keto for Other Health Conditions

Diabetes

While the ketogenic diet has gained recognition for its potential role in cancer management, its benefits extend far beyond oncology. In fact, keto has shown remarkable promise in addressing various other health conditions, and one of the most notable is diabetes.

Diabetes, a chronic condition characterized by high blood sugar levels, affects millions of people worldwide. It's a complex disease with serious health implications, but the ketogenic diet offers a potential solution that's both effective and sustainable.

How Keto Helps Manage Diabetes:

1. **Reduced Carbohydrate Intake:** The cornerstone of the ketogenic diet is a drastic reduction in carbohydrates, the primary culprits behind blood sugar spikes. By minimizing carbs, you prevent those sudden surges and crashes in blood glucose levels, promoting greater stability and control.

2. **Improved Insulin Sensitivity:** Insulin is a hormone that helps your body use glucose for energy. In diabetes, your cells become resistant to insulin, making it difficult to regulate blood sugar levels. Keto has been shown to improve insulin sensitivity, allowing your body to utilize glucose more efficiently and reducing the need for medication in some cases.

3. **Weight Loss:** Obesity is a major risk factor for type 2 diabetes, and shedding excess weight can significantly improve blood sugar control. The ketogenic diet is naturally low in calories and high in satiating fats, making it easier to achieve and maintain a healthy weight.

4. **Reduced Inflammation:** Chronic inflammation is a hallmark of diabetes and contributes to its complications. The ketogenic diet has powerful anti-inflammatory effects, helping to protect your body from the damaging effects of this chronic condition.

5. **Improved Blood Lipid Profile:** Diabetes often comes with an increased risk of heart disease, largely due to abnormal blood lipid levels. Keto can help improve your lipid profile by lowering triglycerides, increasing HDL (good) cholesterol, and improving the size and density of LDL (bad) cholesterol particles.

the power of keto to manage your diabetes, improve your quality of life, and potentially reduce your reliance on medication.

Heart Disease

While the ketogenic diet may not be the first thing that comes to mind when you think of heart health, emerging research suggests that it may hold significant promise for those dealing with heart disease or looking to prevent it.

Now, I know what you're thinking. Isn't keto all about fat? And isn't fat bad for your heart? It's a common misconception, but the truth is, not all fats are created equal.

The ketogenic diet emphasizes healthy fats like those found in avocados, olive oil, nuts, and fatty fish. These fats can actually improve your cholesterol levels, reduce inflammation, and lower your risk of heart disease.

How Keto Benefits Heart Health:

1. **Improved Cholesterol Profile:** Research shows that keto can significantly raise HDL (the "good" cholesterol), lower triglycerides, and improve the size and density of LDL (the "bad" cholesterol) particles, making them less likely to clog your arteries.

2. **Weight Loss:** Obesity is a major risk factor for heart disease. The ketogenic diet's focus on healthy fats and protein can help you shed excess pounds, reducing the strain on your heart and improving its function.

3. **Reduced Inflammation:** Chronic inflammation plays a significant role in the development and progression of heart disease. The ketogenic diet has been shown to have potent anti-inflammatory effects, helping to protect your heart and blood vessels.

4. **Blood Sugar Control:** High blood sugar levels can damage your blood vessels and increase your risk of heart disease. Keto can help regulate blood sugar levels and improve insulin sensitivity, which is beneficial for both heart health and diabetes prevention.

5. **Reduced Blood Pressure:** Some studies suggest that the ketogenic diet may help lower blood pressure, another key risk factor for heart disease.

High Blood Pressure

High blood pressure, often called the "silent killer," is a major risk factor for heart disease, stroke, and other serious health issues. But what if a simple dietary change could help you manage this condition and improve your overall health? That's where the ketogenic diet comes into play.

Now, you might be wondering, "How can a diet rich in fat be good for my heart and blood pressure?" It's a fair question, and the answer lies in the type of fat you're consuming.

The ketogenic diet focuses on healthy fats like those found in avocados, olive oil, nuts, and fatty fish. These fats can actually help lower your blood pressure and improve your heart health.

How Keto Can Help Lower Blood Pressure:

1. **Weight Loss:** Excess weight is a major contributor to high blood pressure. The ketogenic diet's emphasis on satiating fats and protein can help you shed those extra pounds, taking the strain off your cardiovascular system.

2. **Insulin Sensitivity:** Insulin resistance, a common problem in people with high blood pressure, can make it harder for your body to regulate blood pressure. Keto has been shown to improve insulin sensitivity, which can lead to lower blood pressure.

3. **Electrolyte Balance:** The ketogenic diet can help regulate your electrolyte balance, especially sodium and potassium, which are crucial for maintaining healthy blood pressure levels.

4. **Reduced Inflammation:** Chronic inflammation can damage blood vessels and contribute to high blood pressure. The ketogenic diet's anti-inflammatory properties can help protect your blood vessels and lower your risk of hypertension.

5. **Improved Blood Vessel Function:** Some studies suggest that the ketogenic diet may improve the function of your blood vessels, allowing them to relax and dilate more easily, which can lead to lower blood pressure.

Combining Keto with Other Therapies: A Holistic Approach

The ketogenic diet is a powerful tool in its own right, but when combined with other therapies, it can create a synergistic effect that enhances overall well-being and potentially improves outcomes for cancer patients. This holistic approach recognizes that health is multifaceted and requires a multi-pronged strategy for optimal results.

Think of it like a team effort. Just as a sports team combines the strengths of different players to achieve victory, combining keto with other therapies can leverage the unique benefits of each approach to support your body's healing process.

Here's a closer look at how keto can complement various therapies:

1. **Conventional Cancer Treatments:** Chemotherapy, radiation therapy, and surgery are the cornerstones of cancer treatment, but they can often come with harsh side effects like fatigue, nausea, and loss of appetite. The ketogenic diet may help mitigate these side effects by providing a steady source of energy from ketones, reducing inflammation, and improving overall nutritional status. Some studies even suggest that keto may enhance the effectiveness of certain cancer treatments by making cancer cells more vulnerable.

2. **Targeted Therapies and Immunotherapy:** These newer treatments focus on specific molecules or pathways involved in cancer growth and development. While promising, they can also have side effects. The ketogenic diet may help manage these side effects and potentially enhance the effectiveness of these therapies by creating a less hospitable environment for cancer cells.

3. **Complementary and Alternative Therapies:** Many cancer patients turn to complementary and alternative therapies like acupuncture, massage therapy, and mindfulness practices to manage

stress, reduce pain, and improve quality of life. The ketogenic diet can complement these therapies by providing a solid nutritional foundation for overall health and well-being.

4. **Lifestyle Modifications:** Exercise, stress management, and adequate sleep are all crucial components of a healthy lifestyle, especially for cancer patients. The ketogenic diet can support these lifestyle modifications by improving energy levels, reducing fatigue, and promoting mental clarity.

Important Considerations:

While combining keto with other therapies can be beneficial, it's important to approach this holistic strategy with caution and under the guidance of your healthcare team. They can help you determine the best approach for your individual needs, monitor your progress, and adjust your treatment plan as needed.

Here are some key things to keep in mind:

- **Timing:** The timing of keto implementation can be crucial, especially when combined with certain treatments. It's important to discuss this with your doctor to ensure optimal results and avoid any potential complications.

- **Medication Interactions:** The ketogenic diet may interact with certain medications, so it's essential to inform your doctor about all the supplements and medications you're taking.

- **Individualized Approach:** Remember, every cancer patient is unique, and what works for one person may not work for another. It's important to tailor your treatment plan to your specific needs and preferences.

- **Open Communication:** Maintain open communication with your healthcare team throughout your journey. Share your experiences, concerns, and questions with them to ensure you're receiving the best possible care.

By combining the ketogenic diet with other therapies and lifestyle modifications, you can create a comprehensive and personalized approach to cancer care that supports your body's natural healing abilities, improves your quality of life, and empowers you to take an active role in your journey towards recovery.

Chapter 7: Stories of Hope: Keto Warriors Share Their Experiences

Medicine is more than just test tubes and treatment plans; it's about real people, their struggles, their triumphs, and their unwavering spirit. In this chapter, we step away from the science and delve into the heart of the ketogenic journey through the eyes of those who have lived it.

These are the stories of ordinary individuals facing extraordinary challenges, who discovered the power of keto to not only survive but thrive in the face of cancer. They are the keto warriors, and their experiences offer a beacon of hope, inspiration, and a reminder that you are not alone.

You'll meet Sarah, a mother of two who used keto to regain her energy and vitality during chemotherapy, allowing her to be present for her children during their most precious years. You'll hear from David, a retired firefighter who found solace in the kitchen, whipping up delicious keto meals that nourished his body and soul.

And you'll get to know Maria, a young woman who turned her cancer diagnosis into a catalyst for personal growth, using keto to fuel her passion for adventure and reclaim her sense of self.

These are just a few of the countless stories of courage, resilience, and transformation that have emerged from the keto community. They are a testament to the power of food as medicine, the strength of the human spirit, and the unwavering hope that can be found even in the darkest of times.

As you read their stories, I invite you to connect with their experiences, to find inspiration in their journeys, and to see the possibilities that await you on your own keto adventure.

Remember, these warriors are not just survivors; they are thrivers. They have embraced the ketogenic diet as a way of life, not just a temporary measure. They have found joy in nourishing their bodies with wholesome foods, and they have discovered a community of support that has lifted them up during their darkest moments.

Their stories are a reminder that cancer doesn't have to define you. It can be a catalyst for change, a chance to prioritize your health, and an opportunity to embrace a new way of living that nourishes your body, mind, and spirit.

So, open your heart and let their stories inspire you. Let their courage fuel your own, and let their hope guide you towards a brighter future. Together, we can rewrite the narrative of cancer and show the world what it means to truly thrive

Chapter 8: Frequently Asked Questions

As you embark on your ketogenic journey, it's natural to have questions. This chapter aims to address some of the most common queries I hear from patients, providing clear, concise answers and practical guidance to help you navigate the keto lifestyle with confidence.

Q: Will the ketogenic diet cure my cancer?

A: The ketogenic diet is not a cure for cancer, but research suggests it may offer potential benefits in managing the disease and improving treatment outcomes. It's important to work closely with your healthcare team to develop a comprehensive treatment plan that includes both conventional and complementary approaches.

Q: Is the ketogenic diet safe for cancer patients?

A: Generally, the ketogenic diet is safe for most cancer patients when properly implemented and monitored. However, it's crucial to consult with your doctor or a registered dietitian to ensure it's appropriate for your individual needs and health conditions.

Q: What are the potential side effects of the ketogenic diet?

A: Some people may experience temporary side effects during the initial transition to ketosis, often referred to as the "keto flu." These can include fatigue, headaches, constipation, and muscle cramps. These symptoms are usually mild and subside within a few days as your body adjusts.

Q: Can I follow the ketogenic diet if I have other health conditions, like diabetes or high blood pressure?

A: The ketogenic diet has shown promise in managing various health conditions, including diabetes and high blood pressure. However, it's important to consult with your doctor to determine if it's appropriate for your specific situation and to monitor any changes in your medication needs.

Q: How do I know if I'm in ketosis?

A: There are several ways to measure ketone levels, including urine strips, blood meters, and breath analyzers. However, the most reliable indicator of ketosis is how you feel. If you're experiencing increased energy, mental clarity, and reduced appetite, it's likely you're in ketosis.

Q: Can I eat fruit on the ketogenic diet?

A: Most fruits are high in carbohydrates and should be limited on keto. However, some berries like strawberries, raspberries, and blueberries can be enjoyed in moderation.

Q: Can I eat out on the ketogenic diet?

A: Yes, you can definitely eat out on keto! Choose restaurants that offer grilled meats, fish, or salads. Ask for sauces and dressings on the side, and substitute starchy sides like potatoes or rice with non-starchy vegetables.

Q: Will the ketogenic diet make me lose weight?

A: Many people experience weight loss on the ketogenic diet, but it's not guaranteed. The diet's focus on healthy fats and protein can help you feel full and satisfied, naturally leading to reduced calorie intake. However, individual results may vary.

Q: Can I exercise on the ketogenic diet?

A: Absolutely! Exercise is encouraged on keto, but it's important to listen to your body and adjust your activity level as needed. Start with gentle exercises and gradually increase intensity as you adapt to the diet.

Q: Where can I find more information and support on the ketogenic diet?

A: There are many online resources and communities dedicated to the ketogenic diet. I recommend joining online forums, reading books and articles written by experts, and seeking guidance from a registered dietitian who specializes in keto.

Keto Food Lists: Your Compass for Navigating the Grocery Store

Think of this chapter as your keto compass, guiding you through the aisles of the grocery store and helping you make informed choices that support your health and well-being. Knowing what to eat and what to avoid is crucial for achieving and maintaining ketosis, especially when navigating the challenges of cancer treatment.

Foods to Embrace on Keto:

- **Healthy Fats:**
  - Avocados and avocado oil
  - Olives and olive oil
  - Coconut oil, milk, and cream
  - Grass-fed butter and ghee
  - Nuts and seeds (almonds, walnuts, pecans, macadamia nuts, chia seeds, flaxseeds)
  - Nut butters (almond butter, peanut butter)
  - Fatty fish (salmon, mackerel, sardines, tuna)

- **Protein:**
  - Meat (grass-fed beef, lamb, pork, bison)
  - Poultry (chicken, turkey)
  - Fish and seafood (salmon, tuna, shrimp, scallops)
  - Eggs
  - Full-fat dairy (Greek yogurt, cheese, heavy cream)

- **Non-Starchy Vegetables:**
  - Leafy greens (spinach, kale, lettuce)
  - Cruciferous vegetables (broccoli, cauliflower, Brussels sprouts)
  - Asparagus
  - Zucchini
  - Cucumbers
  - Green beans
  - Bell peppers
  - Mushrooms
  - Onions

- **Low-Sugar Fruits (in moderation):**

o Berries (strawberries, raspberries, blueberries)

o Lemons and limes

- **Other:**

  o Herbs and spices

  o Bone broth

  o Unsweetened coffee and tea

  o Dark chocolate (85% cocoa or higher)

Foods to Avoid on Keto:

- **Grains:**

  o Bread, pasta, rice, cereal

  o Oats, quinoa, barley

  o Baked goods

- **Sugary Foods:**

  o Candy, cookies, cake

  o Soda, juice, sweetened beverages

o Honey, maple syrup, agave

- **Starchy Vegetables:**

  o Potatoes, corn, peas

  o Sweet potatoes, yams

  o Winter squash

- **High-Sugar Fruits:**

  o Bananas, grapes, mangoes, pineapples

  o Dried fruit

- **Legumes:**

  o Beans, lentils, chickpeas

- **Processed Foods:**

  o Packaged snacks, processed meats

  o Artificial sweeteners

- **Low-Fat and Diet Products:**

  o These often contain hidden sugars and unhealthy additives

Navigating the Grocery Store:

When shopping for keto-friendly foods, focus on the outer aisles of the grocery store, where you'll find fresh produce, meat, fish, and dairy. Read labels carefully and avoid products with added sugar, unhealthy oils, and artificial ingredients.

Conclusion

A Final Word: Your Journey to Thriving

As you close this book, my hope is that you feel a renewed sense of empowerment and hope. The ketogenic diet is not just a dietary change; it's a lifestyle shift that can profoundly impact your health and well-being, especially as you navigate the challenges of cancer treatment.

Remember, the ketogenic journey is not always easy. There will be bumps in the road, moments of doubt, and perhaps even a few setbacks. But with perseverance, support, and the knowledge you've gained from this book, you can overcome these challenges and emerge stronger than ever.

I encourage you to embrace this journey with an open mind and a hopeful heart. Listen to your body, trust your intuition, and celebrate every small victory along the way. The ketogenic diet is not a magic bullet, but it can be a powerful tool in your arsenal, helping you to fight cancer, reclaim your health, and live a life of vitality and joy.

Your Honest Review Matters:

Your feedback is invaluable to me. If this book has touched your life in any way, please consider leaving a review. Your words of encouragement will not only help others facing similar challenges but will also inspire me to continue my work in empowering cancer patients through the ketogenic diet.

Disclaimer:

The information and recipes in this book are intended for educational and informational purposes only. They are not a substitute for professional medical advice. Always consult with your doctor or a registered dietitian before making any significant changes to your diet or treatment plan.

With warmest wishes for your healing and well-being,

Dr. Kevin Abbott

Made in United States
Troutdale, OR
06/27/2024